CULTURE AND POLITICS IN CANADA

TOWARDS A CULTURE FOR ALL CANADIANS

D. Paul Schafer

WORLD CULTURE PROJECT

ISBN: 1-895661-00-5 (Set)
ISBN: 1-895661-09-9 (Volume 9)

PREFACE

This is a monograph about culture and politics in Canada. It is concerned with one of the most complex and difficult issues in Canadian development of all.

This is a propitious moment to be delving into this issue. Not only is the country going through a period of profound political and cultural transformation, due largely to globalization, the rapidly-changing nature of the Canadian population, the Quebec situation, technological change, and the redistribution of federal, provincial and municipal powers, but also politics and culture hold the key to the country's future development. If the complex connection between culture and politics can be dealt with effectively in the future, it is likely that the country will remain intact and Canadians will experience harmony in their lives together. However, if it cannot be dealt with effectively, it is likely the country will split apart and Canadians will be forced to confront one of the most divisive and disruptive periods in their history.

A great deal more will have to be known about Canadian culture if the complex connection between culture and politics is to be dealt with effectively. In the past, Canadian culture has been viewed in specialized and often elitist terms. This has made it a marginal rather than mainstream activity. For the future, it may be more appropriate to view the country's culture in holistic terms. This would be consistent not only with the comprehensive meaning culture is acquiring in the modern world, but also with the need to bring all provinces, regions, groups and cultures in the country together.

When Canadian culture is viewed in holistic terms, it is a culture of inclusion rather than exclusion. Not only does every Canadian have a fundamental contribution to make to it, but every Canadian has a fundamental stake in it. This makes it a culture of central importance to all

Canadians. It also makes it a culture of vital importance to governments and political parties in all parts of the country.

Like other monographs in the World Culture Project series, the present monograph is intended to be illustrative and exploratory rather than authoritative or definitive in nature. Its purpose is to show how the complex connection between culture and politics has evolved in the past, is dealt with at present, and might be dealt with in the future. It is hoped that this approach will prove helpful in guiding public and private policy and decision-making in the years and decades ahead.

I would like to express my gratitude to Jill Humphries and the advisors to the Canadian Component of the World Culture Project (see appendix) for their valuable contributions to this monograph. While recognizing these contributions, I nevertheless assume responsibility for everything contained in the text.

D. Paul Schafer
Director
World Culture Project
Markham
1998

TABLE OF CONTENTS

Being Canadian means not only having the right and responsibility to shape the future of this country, but also the attendant feelings of ownership and belonging. Our intention must be to build a more inclusive Canada - one in which all Canadians feel at home. We will be able to achieve a truly pan-Canadian identity only when all individuals feel that they are fully part of the whole nation, when they feel included. We are striving to make Canadians confident about their power to shape Canada's future. By empowering our country's parts, we are empowering the whole. Ours will not be so much a nation built on diversity as a nation built out of diversity, a nation lasting, enduring, belonging to all Canadians.[1]

INTRODUCTION

We need to know a great deal more about the reciprocal relation between culture and politics.[1]

John Meisel

If Canadians are to face the future with optimism and enthusiasm rather than pessimism and anxiety, knowledge and understanding of the complex connection between culture and politics will have to be broadened and deepened substantially.

There are many reasons for this, but four in particular are of crucial importance to the country and its citizenry.

In the first place, national unity hinges on it. If Canada is to remain intact and a solution is to be found to the constitutional crisis, a way will have to be found to accommodate the political and cultural needs and aspirations of all provinces, peoples and regions of Canada.[2] If this fails to happen, the country and its citizenry will be compelled to confront the strains of a highly volatile situation and the possibility of splitting apart.

In the second place, Canadian identity depends on it. Canadians can hardly expect to have a strong sense of national identity if the cultural and political imperatives for this are lacking or deficient.

In the third place, Canadian sovereignty demands it. This has become steadily more apparent as a result of the North American Free Trade Agreement and the increased penetration of American culture and American cultural products into Canada. Not only are many of the country's cultural industries owned, operated or controlled by Americans — anywhere from sixty and ninety percent depending on the industry involved and the statistics used[3] — but also aggressive lobbying by American producers,

1

globalization, and recent rulings by the World Trade Organization suggest that these figures could be pushed even higher in the future if aggressive actions are not taken to prevent it.

Finally, Canadian development necessitates it. Canadians cannot expect to maintain a high standard of living and cherished way of life if the cultural and political prerequisites for this are absent. This has become evident as a result of the uncertainty surrounding the Quebec situation and the difficulties involved in resolving the country's political and cultural differences.

A number of questions will have to be addressed in each of these areas if politics and culture are to play a unifying rather than divisive role in Canada in the years and decades ahead.

In the area of national unity, what role should the country's governments play in this process?[4] What objectives should prevail and tools and techniques used? What safeguards should be taken to ensure that the country's governments play a constructive rather than destructive role? And what about the cultural community? What role should it play in keeping the country together? Do cultural agencies like the Canadian Broadcasting Corporation, the Canadian Museum of Civilization, the Canadian Radio-Television and Telecommunications Commission, the National Film Board and the Canada Council for the Arts have a special role to play in the promotion of national unity? If so, how can they execute this role most effectively?

In the area of identity, what responsibilities do the country's governments, the cultural community and the general public have for fostering a strong sense of Canadian identity? How can these responsibilities be discharged most effectively? Do unity and identity work at cross purposes? Was Northrop Frye right when he said, "Assimilating identity to unity produces the empty gestures of cultural nationalism;

assimilating unity to identity produces the kind of provincial isolation which is now called separatism?"[5]

In the area of sovereignty, is Canadian sovereignty best achieved by maintaining close ties with countries like the United States and many European nations with which Canada has had strong traditional ties and historical associations? Or is it best achieved by developing strong ties with other countries, particularly African, Asian and Latin American countries? And what about Canadian culture? Should Canadian culture be protected from too many cultural influences from abroad, especially from the United States? Or should it be exposed to cultures and cultural influences from all parts of the world without the benefit of protective measures or safeguards?

In the area of development, what role do culture and politics now play in Canadian development? What role should they play in the future? Should a market, welfare, or nationalist approach be taken to the development of Canadian culture?[6] What are the implications of this for the country's governments, cultural creators and the general public?

Lurking behind these questions is a set of even more profound questions. What is "Canadian culture?" How is it perceived and defined at present? How should it be perceived and defined in the future? Should the emphasis be placed on developing Canadian culture or on developing many diverse "Canadian cultures?" Are subsidies enough to ensure the realization of Canada's cultural objectives, or are stronger measures required? Is a ministry of culture needed to promote Canadian cultural interests? And perhaps most importantly of all, what role should culture in general — and Canadian culture in particular — play in constitutional change and the country's future development?

As can be seen from these and many other questions which might be posed, there is a whole set of actual and potential contact points connecting culture and politics in Canada. These contact points result from the fact that culture and politics are constantly evolving and impacting on one another. Moreover, their objectives are not the same. Generally speaking, the objectives of culture are creativity, excellence, beauty, truth, and freedom of expression. The objectives of politics are justice, order, equality, access, and participation. There will be times when these objectives converge. When this happens, the welfare and well-being of Canadians is improved in countless ways. However, there will be times when these objectives diverge. When this happens, conflict may be inevitable. For example, the country's cultural community may be struggling to achieve excellence at the same time the country's political community may be struggling to achieve equality. Since excellence requires a heavy concentration of funds and equality requires a broad diffusion of funds, conflict may be inevitable. This same potential for conflict is inherent in the cultural concern with creativity and the political concern with order. Cultural creators may want to stir up Canadian society at the very time politicians and governments want to settle it down. Since "destruction often precedes construction" where creativity is concerned, old structures may have to be torn down before new ones are created. This could put Canada's cultural and political communities on a collision course.

One need only think of the current difficulties separating Quebec and the rest of Canada, the recent encounters with political correctness and the confusion over multiculturalism to confirm the fact that there is a whole set of actual and potential contact points connecting culture and politics in Canada. If the complex connection between culture and politics is to be dealt with effectively in the future, therefore, it will be necessary to broaden and deepen knowledge and understanding of culture and politics and the intimate connection between them. The first step in this process involves expanding awareness of the way the complex connection between culture and politics has evolved in the past. For how this connection has evolved in the past has a fundamental bearing on how it is dealt with at present, and how it might be dealt with in the future.

THE EXPERIENCE OF THE PAST

> It is in a country's interest to support the arts and culture; first, to ensure national survival, but beyond that, as a validation of its history and the life of its people.[1]
>
> Tom Henighan

Throughout most of Canada's history, culture and politics have been separate fields of activity. On the one hand, there have been political needs which have had to be attended to, such as the need for peace, order, government, governance, and the organization of economic, social and human affairs. On the other hand, there have been cultural needs which have had to be addressed, such as the need for expression, meaning and relations with the world. While both sets of needs have been crucial to Canadian survival and well-being, it is difficult to detect a specific connection between them until well into the twentieth century. Where such a connection existed prior to this time, it was usually more implicit than explicit, invisible than visible.

THE PRE CONFEDERATION ERA

The earliest expressions of Indian and Inuit life in Canada illustrate the fact that there is little visible evidence of a specific connection between culture and politics until the present century. There are vivid reminders of the cultural needs of the Indians and the Inuit, as the rock paintings and petroglyphs of the Ojibway, the myths and legends of the Cree, the costumes of the MicMacs, the totem poles of the Haida, the masks of the Kwakiutl, and the stone carvings and prints of the Inuit indicate. There are also vivid reminders of the political needs of these highly inventive peoples, as the powwow, the caucus meeting, the passing of the peace-pipe and the pioneering achievements in democracy and democratic forms of government confirm. What is difficult to detect, however, is a specific connection between these political and cultural requirements.

This same situation holds true for the first French settlers. They had many political needs which had to be attended to, as illustrated by the earliest forms of governance at Port Royal. They also had many cultural needs which had to be addressed, as institutions like the Order of Good Cheer which was created to satisfy the need for food, music, song and dance reveal. It was at this time, for example, that Lescarbot composed the verses of **Les Muses de la Nouvelle France** and wrote **Neptune's Theatre**. What is much less apparent, however, is evidence of a specific connection between these political and cultural activities.

If the French had many political and cultural needs to be attended to from the earliest days of French settlement in North America, these needs were magnified significantly as settlement moved westward from Port Royal to Quebec and Montreal. In both politics and culture, the Church and the Jesuits played a prominent role. By the middle of the seventeenth century, an École des Arts et Métiers had been founded in Quebec to teach painting, sculpting, carpentry and weaving in addition to agriculture. It was to play a significant role in the evolution of early French religious painting, statue-making, silverwork, embroidery, and leather work. Only later, as many other achievements were recorded in sacred music, scholarship, drama, politics, law and government by Quebec's religious sects, political authorities and aristocratic classes, was it realized that the French had laid a solid basis for political and cultural expansion in Canada, as well as throughout the entire North American continent.

Between 1600 and 1867, numerous advances were recorded in the cultural and political life of the country, not only by the French as a result of their high regard for learning, education, the arts, religion and governance, but also by the English, Irish, Scotch, Germans, Ukrainians, Scandinavians, United Empire Loyalists and other peoples who made Canada their home during this time. Most of these advances were achieved as a result of relentless efforts on the part of religious organizations, educational institutions and wealthy elites.

In the cultural field, some of the biggest advances were recorded in the field of music. Both sacred and secular music flourished between 1600 and 1867. Sacred music was performed in most of the churches. It included not only liturgical singing and organ music, but also many large oratorios. Secular music progressed apace. The folk songs of the habitants, trappers and voyageurs of Quebec, as well as the farmers and fishermen of Newfoundland, Nova Scotia and New Brunswick, developed first. Later, bands played an important role, not only for military occasions, religious functions and performances in public squares, but also for theatrical events. When Charles Dickens visited Montreal in 1842, for instance, he saw a play with music performed by the band of the 23rd. Regiment. Music also proved to be an ideal complement to the many dances which were popular at the time, especially cotillions, quadrilles, polkas, mazurkas, square dances, jigs, and hornpipes. There were composers too, like John Quesnel, who wrote several drawing-room operas such as **Colas and Colinette** and a number of plays, as well as Calixa Lavallée who wrote the country's national anthem.

In literature, Nova Scotia and Halifax took the lead. It was in Halifax that the country's oldest literary periodical — the **Nova Scotia Magazine** — was started in 1799. Nova Scotia also had many of the country's first writers, including Oliver Goldsmith, Thomas Haliburton and Joseph Howe. Later, Quebec and Ontario inspired talented writers like Louis Fréchette, Susanna Moodie and Catherine Parr Traill. Many of these writers wrote for magazines and periodicals, such as Montreal's **Literary Garland** which did so much to provide opportunities to aspiring writers by publishing poems, short stories and articles.

Although theatre developed more slowly, it was in an active state of development by the first half of the nineteenth century. Canada's first real theatre opened in Halifax in 1787. By 1816, a professional group was producing plays of a high calibre in Saint John. Although plays such as those of Molière were produced in Quebec prior to this period, the first real theatre built in Quebec was Montreal's Theatre Royal, created in 1826. In the decades to follow, many theatres were built in Upper and Lower Canada to house touring professional groups from England and the United States, as well as to provide opportunities for local resident groups. A solid basis was being laid for Canada's future theatrical expansion at this time.

In painting, Quebec City played the pivotal role, due largely to painters like Légaré, Plamondon, Hamel, Triaud, and others. Following in their footsteps were talented painters like Cornelius Kreighoff and Paul Kane whose works were destined to have an important impact on Canadian painting in the decades to follow. In the crafts, every community had its need for people with creative talents. While many goods had to be imported from abroad, many had to be fashioned in Canada. As a result, skilled artisans — who could make everything from household items to religious relics — were in great demand. Architectural and urban requirements also imposed challenges and provided opportunities. Churches, schools, farm houses, homes and other buildings had to be built, thereby creating a demand for architects, carpenters, stonemasons, carvers, designers and town planners.

Countless political requirements also had to be attended to in the period between 1600 and 1867.

Champlain played a crucial role in the early part of this period by governing the French colony at Quebec and guiding exploration and settlement from Quebec to Montreal and beyond. The seminal role he provided paved the way for the establishment of a royal system of government and the creation of New France as a crown colony in 1663.

Included in this system were: a governor who was charged with responsibility for defence and was the king's representative in the colony; an intendant who was responsible for industry, trade and administration; and a bishop who was responsible for religious matters and education. In the years to follow, this rapidly-evolving system of government, which was not without its problems, was developed by Jean Talon and Count Frontenac. Jean Talon laid the basis for New France's economic and seigniorial system by encouraging crafts, farming and local industry along the Saint Lawrence River. Count Frontenac laid the basis for French expansion westward by encouraging exploration from the Mississippi River to the Gulf of Mexico, as well as by expanding the fur-trading boundaries of New France throughout the North America continent. By the early 18th. century, the empire of New France extended from Hudson's Bay to the Gulf of Mexico and Newfoundland to the Great Lakes.

Conflict between the French and the English was inevitable as the English presence in North America intensified throughout the 18th. century. North America in general, and the northern half of it in particular, proved to be the battleground for many battles between France and England as they vied for power in Europe and generally throughout the world. While peace sometimes prevailed in the first half of the 18th. century, the peace was broken in 1754 when France and England became embroiled in the Seven Years War. This lead to the loss of Louisbourg by the French in 1758, the battle on the Plains of Abraham in 1759, the Treaty of Paris which ceded French possessions in North America to Great Britain in 1763, and the Quebec Act which guaranteed the French system of civil law and the seigniorial system of land tenure in 1774.

Towards the end of the century, this situation was altered in dramatic fashion by conflicts which erupted in the American colonies, the American Revolution, and the inflow of United Empire Loyalists into New Brunswick, Quebec and Ontario. This eventually led to the creation of Upper and Lower Canada, as well as to tensions between Canadians and Americans. These tensions lead to a series of battles between Canadians and Americans, the Treaty of Ghent, which was signed in 1814 to bring the War of 1812 to an end, and a period of rapid expansion for British North America between 1814 and 1867. This period was not without its political problems, however, as evidenced by the conflicts between elected assemblies and legislative councils, the rebellions of Upper and Lower Canada led by William Lyon Mackenzie and Louis-Joseph Papineau in 1837, the appointment of Lord Durham as Governor General for British North America, and the **Durham Report** of 1839. The **Report** recommended the union of Upper and Lower Canada as a step towards assimilation of French Canadians, as well as the granting of responsible government to the colonies.

By the 1850s and early 1860s, it was clear that union of all the colonies in British North America was the only solution to the new set of problems which had emerged. One such problem was the adoption of free trade by the British in 1846; another was the "Manifest Destiny" movement in the United States following conclusion of the American Civil War in 1865; and a final one was the friction encountered as a result of the union of Upper and Lower Canada. In one form or another, these problems, and others, played a powerful role in the passage of the British North America Act of 1867, which brought together the provinces of Nova Scotia, New Brunswick, Quebec and Ontario to form the Dominion of Canada. A new era was unfolding in Canada — an era that had significant implications for culture and politics and the complex connection between them.

CONFEDERATION TO CENTENNIAL

By the time of Confederation, Canada had built up an impressive array of political and cultural achievements. On the political side, there were numerous laws, legislative enactments, political parties and governments. On the cultural side, there were many musical works, dances, stories, plays, paintings, craft objects, architectural edifices, historical sites and unique buildings. While some of these achievements had an indigenous quality about them, most of them were cast squarely in the European tradition. Thus there was a German ring to the music, a Scottish and Irish flair to the dances, a European tinge to the theatre, and an English and French character to the politics, legislative enactments, legal codes and bureaucratic structures.

Although Canada possessed a flourishing political and cultural life by Confederation, culture and politics still existed largely as separate fields of activity and were relatively isolated from one another. While the country's governments were participating in a number of worthwhile cultural undertakings by the time of Confederation, particularly assistance with festivals and establishment of some of the country's first community art galleries and museums, culture was not important enough — or sufficiently differentiated from other fields of activity — to be treated as an activity in its own right in the constitution. Thus, unlike defence, foreign affairs, natural resources, education and civil and property rights which received prominent billing in the British North America Act, culture was not addressed at all in the Act.

This lack of a political designation for culture in the BNA Act has left an indelible mark on culture and politics in Canada. On the one hand, it has meant that all levels of government have been involved in the cultural life of the country in varying degrees. This has had the effect of multiplying the funds available for cultural development, reducing the risk of the piper calling the tune, and producing a system of funding which is more diversified than would have been the case if responsibility for culture had been ceded to a single level of government. On the other hand, it has meant that culture has never been fully addressed as a political responsibility in Canada, largely because there was no real mention of culture in the BNA Act and there is a great deal of uncertainty surrounding the cultural responsibilities of the various levels of government. Surely this helps to explain why cultural considerations have been conspicuous by their absence from the many constitutional discussions and debates of recent years, despite the fact that culture lies at the root of virtually every major problem confronting the country and its citizenry at the present time, be it national unity and identity, sovereignty, development, or relations between Quebec and the rest of Canada.

Despite the fact that culture was not addressed in the BNA Act, pressure was building on governments at all levels by the time of Confederation to get more involved in the cultural life of the country. This pressure centred on the need to conserve and protect the country's rapidly-burgeoning collection of artefacts, monuments, historic sites, manuscripts, masterpieces, documents, films, photographs, paintings, and wilderness areas. In order to respond to this need, numerous galleries, museums, libraries, archives and parks had to be created. It is in the area of heritage, preservation and conservation, therefore, that the first real signs of a specific connection between politics and culture begin to manifest themselves in Canada. It is a connection that has steadily evolved and intensified ever since.

The federal government was the first to respond to this pressure in a concerted and systematic way. Between the late 1880s and the early 1930s, it established a number of institutions such as the Library of Parliament, the Dominion Archives, the National Gallery of Art, the Canadian Motion Picture Bureau and the Historic Sites and Monuments Board to conserve and protect the country's rapidly-growing cultural heritage. These institutions served to complement the involvement of the federal government in other fields of cultural endeavour, such as the organization of exhibitions, trade fairs and tours by artists and arts organizations, purchase of artistic works, support for multicultural activities like the New Canadian Folk Song and Handicraft Festival which was staged in Winnipeg in 1928, and numerous commissions for monuments, coins, plaques and paintings. In the formulation and implementation of these activities, prime ministers like Wilfrid Laurier and Mackenzie King, and governors general and political figures like the Earl of Dufferin, Lord

Bessborough, the Marquis of Lorne and Lord Grey, played a prominent role.[2] Not only did they play a forceful role in founding several key Canadian cultural institutions, such as the Royal Canadian Academy of Arts, the Royal Society of Canada and the Dominion Drama Festival, but also they recognized that culture possesses the potential to make a vital contribution to national unity and identity.

This penetration by the federal government into the cultural life of the country is important for two reasons. First, it laid the foundation for Canada's present system of heritage preservation and conservation. Second, it set the stage for a "top-down approach" to Canadian cultural development. It is an approach that has been characteristic of Canadian cultural development ever since, despite the fact that the provinces and municipalities have been increasingly involved in the cultural life of the country over the last few decades.

While a solid basis was being laid for Canada's heritage system in the public sector between the late 1880s and early 1930s, a strong foundation was being laid for the country's arts system in the private sector.[3] In music, many important musical organizations were created between 1880 and 1930, including the Montreal Symphony, the Toronto Symphony, the Toronto Conservatory of Music and the Vancouver Symphony Society. In theatre, Winnipeg had four theatres by 1990 — the Winnipeg Theatre, the Winnipeg Opera House, the Dominion Theatre and the Walter Theatre — thereby establishing its reputation as the gateway to culture in western Canada and a real pioneer in the country's theatrical development. Although much of the theatrical touring was done by British and American companies, thereby limiting the development of Canadian talent and the realization of an indigenous repertoire, many amateur groups were formed and flourished during this period, including the Little Theatre Association, the Shakespeare Society, and the Players Club at Hart House. In addition, the Dominion Drama Festival was founded in 1932. It played a seminal role in Canadian theatrical development until well into the 1960s by providing a showcase for dramatic talent and providing the only real coast-to-coast link for the country's theatrical community. The development of service associations continued apace. By the early 1930s, many service associations had been established, including the Royal Architectural Institute, the Société des Écrivains Canadiens, the Canadian Authors' Association, the Sculptors' Society of Canada, the Canadian Society of Painters in Water Colour, and others.

The struggle to create and sustain these institutions and activities was a demanding one. Since audiences were small and funding was limited, a great deal of dedication, hard work and sacrifice was required on the part of the country's artists, arts organizations, and expanding network of administrators and volunteers. It was this same kind of challenge which confronted the Group of Seven, who were struggling at this time to establish themselves as professional artists capable of producing the indigenous forms of artistic expression which would help Canadians understand their own cultural reality.

While Canada's cultural community and the federal government were busy laying the foundation for the country's present arts and heritage systems, a development in the field of broadcasting contributed admirably to this process. It had the effect of drawing the federal government more fully into the cultural life of the country, as well as providing the cultural community with a badly-needed stimulus at the right time.

This development was the establishment of the Canadian Broadcasting Corporation (CBC). It was created as a Crown corporation by the federal government in 1936, following a period of intense lobbying on the part of the Canadian Radio League, the passage of the Radio Act of 1927, and the creation of the Royal Commission on Radio (the Aird Commission) in 1928.

The CBC was created "to develop a national broadcasting service for all Canadians in both official languages which would be primarily Canadian in content and character."[4] The decision to create it was an historic one — one which has had a profound effect on Canada, Canadians, and Canadian development. For one thing, it indicated that the federal government had decided to combat American cultural penetration into Canada by encouraging domestic activity rather than impeding foreign activity. With few exceptions, this course of action has been followed by successive federal governments right up to the present day. For another thing, it demonstrated a preference for dealing with complex administrative problems in the cultural field largely by creating autonomous agencies at arm's length from government and the political process rather than through direct involvement on the part of government departments and ministries. By and large, this precedent has been followed ever since, as the establishment of cultural agencies like the National Film Board (NFB), the Canada Council for the Arts, the National Arts Centre (NAC), Telefilm Canada, and the Canadian Radio-Television and Telecommunications Commission (CRTC) readily reveal. Finally, and perhaps most importantly, it revealed an awareness at the highest political level that cultural problems cannot be solved exclusively by private sector activity, occasional grants, or random public actions. Public sector involvement was needed on a sustained and systematic basis if Canada was to evolve a viable system of cultural development and a dynamic cultural life.

What was it about the CBC in those early years which projected it into a prominent position in the cultural life of the country? Three things: first, the ability to link the country together from coast to coast; second, the ability to produce dynamic and diversified programming; and third, the ability to provide economic and artistic opportunities for Canada's cultural creators when they needed them the most. For no sooner was the CBC established and functioning than the country's cultural community was compelled to provide it with the ideas, talents and programmes which were needed to operate effectively. By responding in this way, the CBC acted as an incredible stimulus to Canadian creativity in particular and Canadian cultural development in general.

In drama, the CBC's **Stage** and **Wednesday Night Series** — for which special stock companies of actors, actresses and writers had to be created — produced everything from specially-commissioned Canadian plays to the works of Shakespeare, Ibsen, Tolstoy, Molière, Shaw and Marlowe. Many well-known Canadian actors and writers profited from these ambitious undertakings, including John Drainie, Christopher Plummer, William Hutt, Lorne Greene, Barry Morse, W.O. Mitchell, Mazo de la Roche, Robertson Davies, Len Peterson and Lister Sinclair. In music, many symphonic, choral and chamber concerts were presented, as were countless recitals, prom concerts and programmes like **Singing Stars of Tomorrow** which featured such artists as Maureen Forrester, Jon Vickers, Lois Marshall, Giles Lamontagne and Marie José Forgues. Just as stock companies had to be created to perform theatrical works, so the CBC Orchestra and CBC Opera Company had to be created to perform musical and operatic works. To the list should be added programmes like **The Happy Gang, La Famille Plouffe, Opportunity Knocks, Rawhide, Canadian Theatre of the Air**, and others. Small wonder the CBC is recognized as one of the most important cultural institutions in the country.

If the CBC was to be the ears of Canada, the NFB was to be its eyes. At least that was the opinion of John Grierson, the NFB's founding director, who contended that "the National Film Board will be the eyes of Canada. It will, through a national use of cinema, see Canada and see it whole."

When it was established at the outbreak of World War II in 1939, few thought the NFB, with its mandate to "produce, distribute and promote the production and distribution of films designed to interpret Canada to Canadians and to other nations," would become one of the most productive and respected public film agencies in the world. Who would have guessed, for example, that the NFB would make many valuable contributions to the war effort and the art of film, including documentaries, cinema verité, animation, multi-screen viewing, and the training of thousands of French and English film-makers and technicians. Moreover, who would have guessed that millions of NFB films would been seen each year throughout the world, due largely to aggressive distribution policies and centres strategically located in different parts of the globe.

While the federal government was busy creating the institutions and initiatives which were needed to respond to the difficulties posed by communications, broadcasting and film, Canada's cultural community was busy creating the resources which were needed to bring about changes on another front.

Despite the awesome geographical challenges confronting Canada's cultural community, there have been times when it has acted with remarkable cohesion and strength. One such time was the presentation of the **Artists' Brief** in 1944 to the Special Committee of the House of Commons on Reconstruction and Re-establishment (the Turgeon Committee). The **Brief** was prepared by an assembly of the country's leading artists and arts administrators. It was spearheaded by the Canadian Arts Council, now the Canadian Conference of the Arts (CCA). According to one observer, it was "one of the most businesslike statements ever submitted to a parliamentary committee. Their story was neat, direct and understandable. No redundancy. No exaggeration. No class-consciousness, axe-grinding, self-seeking argument. Nothing but honest common sense, clearly stated and sincerely argued."[5]

The **Brief** called for many measures to improve cultural life in Canada, including a government body to provide financial assistance, effective copyright protection for artists, improvements in town planning and industrial design, promotion of Canadian art abroad, and construction of a number of community arts centres across the country. This latter proposal was particularly attractive to the members of the Reconstruction and Re-establishment Committee because it would have provided an effective link between amateurs and professionals, made all levels of government responsible for culture, and addressed difficult problems like centralist domination, the country's vast size and geography, and reliance on foreign producers, organizers and philanthropists.[6]

A number of factors were conspiring at the end of World War II to make the cultural community's hope for more government support for culture a reality. In the first place, there was the rapid growth of the cultural field itself, spurred on by the euphoria over the termination of the war, the return of the troops from abroad, the excitement of post-war recovery, and the prospect of peace. Secondly, there was the movement among artists and arts administrators to break the centuries-old shackles of amateurism, and, in Quebec, the publication of **Refus global** which called for the modernization and liberalization of Quebec through freeing of the arts from the traditionalism of the Church and the conventionalism of education. Finally, there was the pressure for more financial assistance for the arts, better utilization of the country's creative capabilities, more professionalism, and more effective use of artistic and financial resources.

These factors, and others, set the stage for one of the greatest cultural landmarks in Canadian history. This landmark was the **Royal Commission on National Development in the Arts, Letters and Sciences**, or the Massey-Lévesque Commission. It was established by the federal government in 1949 to respond to pressure which was building in the cultural community and across the country for a major assessment of the present state and future prospects for the country's cultural development. For the first time in Canadian history, culture had become sufficiently important — and sufficiently differentiated from other fields of activity like education and religion — to warrant a full-scale investigation of it.

In general terms, the Commission was directed to examine "the needs and desires of the citizens in relation to science, literature, art, music, drama, films and broadcasting." More specifically, it was charged with responsibility for making recommendations concerning broadcasting, higher education, the cultural activities of government departments and agencies, international relations, and the work of voluntary organizations. In the course of its work, the Commission revealed many fundamental deficiencies in Canadian cultural life. It also revealed an appalling lack of Canadian content in virtually every field of artistic, academic and scientific endeavour. This made it difficult to come to grips with the Commission's two principal preoccupations: how to allocate public funds to worthwhile cultural undertakings without stifling private initiative; and how to distribute assistance in a manner consistent with the federal structure of government and the regional diversity of the country.

In coming to grips with these concerns, the Commission demonstrated a remarkable vision when it released its **Report** in 1951.[7] The **Report** was predicated on the conviction that the arts, education and culture have a crucial role to play in the maintenance of a strong and united Canada. It was within this context that the Commission made a series of recommendations which were destined to have a profound impact on the cultural life of the country, even if a considerable period of time was to elapse before some of these recommendations were implemented. Most importantly, it recommended creation of a Canada Council for the Encouragement of the Arts, Letters, Humanities and Social Sciences, promotion of Canadian artistic and academic interests abroad, and establishment of a major scholarship programme. As important as these recommendations were, they should not be allowed to obscure the fact that there were many other important recommendations contained in the Massey-Lévesque **Report**, including granting authority to the CBC to license private broadcasting and control television, expanding federal cultural agencies, and more employment of domestic talent.

While reaction to the Massey-Lévesque **Report** was enthusiastic in most parts of the country, reaction to it was mixed in Quebec.[8] There, some saw it as a spur to cultural development while others saw it as a threat to Quebec's ability to create cultural programmes and institutions of its own choosing:

> The Massey-Lévesque Report, as it came to be known in Québec, divided the province's intellectuals into two main camps. The first group maintained that the soundest way to protect the cultural development of Québec was to let the *federal* government defend Canadian culture from the influences pouring in from the United States. The second group felt that *Québec* must develop its own cultural institutions, parallel to those being established by Ottawa, and that the province should exercise exclusive jurisdiction in this field to avoid becoming a mere tributary of the central source.[9]

This division of the intellectuals of Quebec into two main camps had an important bearing on the creation of Quebec's first separatist political party — the L'Alliance laurentienne — which eventually contributed to the creation of the Parti Québécois in 1968.[10] For the first time in the country's history, there were signs that culture could act as a divisive as well as unifying force. If the cultural needs of Canada, the provinces and especially Quebec were to be dealt with effectively, much more time and attention would have to be devoted to the role that governments play in cultural life and the conflicting demands of political and cultural centralization and decentralization.

While action on many of the recommendations contained in the Massey-Lévesque **Report** was commenced shortly after the **Report** was released in 1951, six years were to elapse before the implementation of the main recommendation concerning creation of the Canada Council. And this only happened, according to many, because two wealthy benefactors from the Maritimes died and left substantial bequests to the federal government which appeared to be ideal for the purpose.

In retrospect, the reasons for a considerable lapse of time are not difficult to discern. It was one thing for the federal government to accept responsibility for cultural agencies of its own creation, such as the CBC and NFB, as well as for conservation and preservation of the country's cultural heritage. It was quite another for the government to accept responsibility for supporting cultural organizations and institutions outside government. Not only would this open up a whole new era in governmental and political involvement in the cultural life of the country, but also it would establish a precedent future governments would be expected to honour. Yet, this is exactly what the federal government was being pressured to do by the cultural community and committed individuals and institutions across the country.

In the end, the pressure proved to be too much. In 1956, Prime Minister Louis Saint Laurent announced the decision to create the Canada Council at the National Conference on Higher Education in Ottawa. In making the announcement, Saint Laurent said:

> An extensive national cultural policy has been gradually developed...although many Canadians may feel that, in certain sectors, it has been too modest and timid.... This policy has been aimed at strengthening and developing our main cultures without attempting to impose either of them upon any Canadians. It is based upon the principle that private initiative has the main responsibility in most aspects of our cultural development. It has provided financial assistance to individuals, voluntary organizations and institutions in order to support them without attempting, however, to control their activities. Finally this policy has also included the setting up of several public agencies which were deemed essential for the development and the adequate expression of our cultural life. [11]

The Canada Council was created in 1957 with a mandate "to foster and promote the study and enjoyment of, and the production of, works in the arts, humanities and social sciences in Canada." This confirmed two things without a shadow of a doubt. First, public support for arts organizations and activities outside government was a legitimate political responsibility. With this came official recognition of the fact that artists and arts organizations deserve financial support from government due to the difficulty of making ends meet in the marketplace. Second, governments have no business making decisions or judgements about the allocation of funds for artistic and cultural purposes. With this came official recognition that funding for the arts should be as free as possible from political manipulation and governmental control.

When the Canada Council was created, it was modelled along the lines of the Arts Council of Great Britain. Whereas the Arts Council of Great Britain was created to provide public funding for the arts, however, the Canada Council was created to provide public funding for the arts, social sciences and humanities. This was consistent with the Massey-Lévesque Commission's mandate to examine the arts, social sciences and humanities in Canada. The country's provincial governments were probably only too delighted to see the federal government assuming some responsibility for the financing of higher education in Canada, especially if it was provided through an autonomous agency rather than a government department in view of the provinces' constitutional authority over education.

Creation of the Canada Council is important for many reasons. First, it confirmed the principle that cultural agencies should be created at arm's length from government and the political process to deal with particular types of cultural problems such as funding and programming. This was consistent with the creation of the CBC and NFB as autonomous agencies with a great deal of authority and control over their affairs, as well as with practices and policies prevalent in countries like Great Britain. For the Arts Council of Great Britain was also created at arm's length from government and the political process, due largely to the conviction that governments have no business involving themselves directly in the cultural affairs of countries.

Second, it sanctioned the practice of looking to Great Britain and Western Europe generally for solutions to Canadian cultural problems. The reason for this is not difficult to detect. Not only was it easier to capitalize on tailor-made solutions to problems than to search for indigenous solutions to them, but also Western European countries and especially countries like Great Britain had a great deal of experience and expertise in dealing with the types of problems encountered by governments in the cultural field.

Finally, it reinforced the practice of treating "the arts" and "culture" as synonymous for political purposes. For despite the fact that the Canada Council included the social sciences and humanities in its mandate, it was a well-known fact that education was a provincial matter by constitution. This had the effect of promoting an artistic definition of culture in Canada, although there were probably many Canadians who believed culture had much more to do with sports, recreation and relationships with "the land" than the arts.

From the outset, the Canada Council was concerned with two matters of crucial importance to artistic development in Canada. The first was creation of the highest standards of excellence. The second was creation of a corps of professional artists and arts organizations capable of meeting these standards. While this approach downplayed the demand side of the arts, the need for more Canadian content, community cultural development and arts education, even the staunchest critics were forced to admit the Council had little alternative in the early years. A corps of professional artists and arts organizations and high standards of excellence were needed if the Council was to be successful in fulfilling its mandate.

The Council was created just in time. For a new wave of artists and arts organizations was appearing on the scene. Included among the organizations were the Stratford Shakespearean Festival, the Théâtre du Nouveau Monde, the Théâtre du Rideau Vert, the Manitoba Theatre Centre, the Shaw Festival, Les Grand Ballet Canadiens, the Royal Winnipeg Ballet, the National Ballet of Canada, the Canadian Opera Company, and others. Included among the artists were Jean-Paul Riopelle, Marcel Barbeau, Jack Shadbolt, Mordecai Richler, Harry Somers, Harold Town, Jean-Louis Roux, Glenn Gould, Anne Hébert, and others. There were training institutions too, like the National Theatre School in Montreal and the National Ballet School in Toronto.

Many factors combined to make the period from the creation of the Canada Council in 1957 to the late 1960s one of the most prolific periods in Canadian cultural history.

Governments were growing rapidly and economic expansion was placing Canadians in a much stronger position to buy artistic products and purchase tickets to artistic events. It was also placing governments in a much stronger position to increase their funding for cultural purposes. The phenomenal growth of educational institutions across the country made it possible to introduce many more courses in the arts, as well as to expand residency and teaching opportunities for Canadian artists. Then there were the changes taking place in the Canadian population. Canada's younger and better educated labour force was being supplemented by immigrants from Europe and elsewhere in the world who brought with them new artistic interests and tastes. Finally, there was television. It appeared in 1951 with the opening of CBFT in Montreal and CBLT in Toronto. It grew rapidly. By the mid 1960s, the impact of television on the country, like radio before it, had been phenomenal, due largely to its rapid expansion, its programming requirements, and its novelty. A new generation of writers, actors, actresses, composers and musicians was needed to turn these possibilities into realities.

With favourable political, economic, educational, demographic and technological conditions, opportunities really started to open up for the country's performing, exhibiting and media talents. These opportunities were augmented by another significant factor. Pressure was building on provincial governments and the provinces generally to get more involved in the country's cultural life.

Given Quebec's position at the cutting edge of Canadian cultural development — a position it has consistently maintained from the earliest days of French settlement in North America to the present day — it was the first to respond to this pressure. In 1961, the Government of Quebec established the Ministère des Affaires culturelles as the first "cultural ministry" in Canada. This was consistent with the approach taken in France, where, unlike Great Britain, there was a marked preference for direct government involvement in cultural development and the creation of government departments rather than arm's length cultural agencies. It was also consistent with the profound changes going on in Quebec society, including "la révolution tranquille" and the shift that was taking place in education from Church to State.

No sooner was the Ministère des Affaires culturelles created than it identified a need to establish several new cultural institutions, including l'Office de la langue française, le Département du Canada français d'outre-frontière, le Conseil provincial des arts, and la Commission des monuments historiques. It was clear from these initiatives that a broader view of culture was emerging in Quebec compared to other provinces in Canada. It was a view that underlined the vital connection between culture, the arts, education, language, history, people, heritage and politics. This view was asserted in the Laporte Commission's **White Paper on Culture**.[12] While the paper was not released due to the defeat of the Lesage government in 1966 and only became available on an unofficial basis later, it emphasized the crucial importance of language, culture and civilization to Quebec's future development. Moreover, it symbolized the first attempt by a government anywhere in the country to identify the principles, objectives and guidelines on which cultural development and policy should be based. Many of these principles, objectives and guidelines were stated in the **Rioux Report** of 1966 which proposed sweeping changes in the way the arts and culture were taught in Quebec schools.[13] These developments helped to pave the way for the many political, administrative and policy changes aimed at strengthening culture, language, history, education and the arts which have taken place in Quebec since the mid 1960s.

While other provinces were responding less actively to the need for greater public commitment to culture, they were nevertheless engaging in many undertakings which were destined to have an important impact on the country's cultural development. In the Atlantic region, for example, the Government of Nova Scotia was accelerating its support for the arts and culture through the Department of Education, the Government of Prince Edward Island was channelling support through the Charlottetown Confederation Centre, the Government of Newfoundland was laying the foundation for major cultural centres in Saint John's and Cornerbrook, and the Government of New Brunswick was establishing a Cultural Affairs Division in the Premier's Office. Elsewhere, the Government of Ontario created the Ontario Arts Council in 1963, the Government of Manitoba created the Manitoba Arts Council in 1965, and the Government of British Columbia created the Centennial Cultural Fund in 1967. These initiatives complemented earlier developments in Saskatchewan and Alberta where the Saskatchewan Arts Board and the Cultural Development Branch in Alberta had been established two decades earlier, thereby establishing the reputation of these provinces as real pioneers in public cultural administration in Canada. By 1967, the pattern had been set. Rather than relinquishing the cultural field to the federal government, the provincial governments had decided to play an important role in Canadian cultural development of their own. This role was not limited to the creation of cultural departments, cultural branches in other ministries, or cultural agencies at arm's length from the political process. It also included support programmes for individuals and institutions outside government.

These changes in provincial cultural infrastructure did not go unnoticed in Ottawa. If numerous infrastructural changes were required at the provincial level, they were also required at the federal level. Not only had many new institutions been created since the release of the Massey-Lévesque Report in 1951, but also many other changes had taken place in the way cultural development was conducted in the country.

Following release of the **Report of the Royal Commission on Government Organization** (the Glassco Commission) in 1962,[14] the federal government introduced a series of revisions to the **Secretary of State Act** in 1963.[15] These revisions were designed to bring all federal cultural activities under the responsibility of a single minister. Without naming it as such, the government had created a Department of Cultural Affairs, complete with a minister who was expected to spend the bulk of his or her time addressing cultural issues and problems. Maurice Lamontagne was appointed Secretary of State in 1964 and immediately commenced a dialogue with the country's arts community. It was a dialogue destined to have important implications for the government, the arts, artists, arts organizations and service associations like the Canadian Conference of the Arts, which, by this time, was performing an extremely valuable function by providing a public forum for discussion on cultural matters.

These developments, like many others taking place across the country, occurred at the same time that another Canadian cultural landmark was in the making. This landmark was the **Royal Commission on Bilingualism and Biculturalism**.

What makes the Royal Commission on Bilingualism and Biculturalism a landmark is the fact that it set in motion a chain of events which led to Canada's current policy of multiculturalism within a bilingual framework.[16] Here is how it came about. When the Commission was established in 1963, it was predicated on the conviction that Canada was basically a bilingual and bicultural country involving two founding peoples — French and English. While many people of non-English and non- French background were prepared to accept the conviction that Canada was a "bilingual" country by virtue of the fact that French and English were the two major languages of Canada, they were not prepared to accept the conviction that Canada was a "bicultural" country. The reason for this is clear. Many people of non-English and non-French background had made, and continued to make, valuable contributions to Canadian development in general and Canadian cultural development in particular. These contributions demanded recognition and attention in an official, public sense as well as an unofficial, private sense.

Recognition of this fact eventually caused the Commission to abandon the notion of "biculturalism" in favour of "multiculturalism." When the Commission released its **Report**,[17] Book IV was devoted almost entirely to the contributions made by ethnic groups and communities of non- British and non-French extraction.[18] This set the stage for the Government's official response to Book IV of the **Report**. In 1971, it proclaimed Canada's official policy of multiculturalism within a bilingual framework:

> We believe that cultural pluralism is the very essence of Canadian identity. Every ethnic group has the right to preserve and develop its own culture and values within the Canadian context. To say that we have two official languages is not to say we have two official cultures, and no particular culture is more official than another. A policy of multiculturalism must be a policy for all Canadians.[19]

The Government went on to state that public support and encouragement would be provided to:

> ...the various cultures and ethnic groups that give structure and vitality to our society. They will be encouraged to share their cultural expression and values with other Canadians and so contribute to a richer life for us all.... In implementing a policy of multiculturalism within a bilingual framework, the government will provide support in four ways:
>
> First, resources permitting, the government will seek to assist all Canadian cultural groups that have

demonstrated a desire and effort to continue to develop a capacity to grow and contribute to Canada, and a clear need for assistance, the small and weak groups no less than the strong and highly organized.

Second, the government will assist members of all cultural groups to overcome cultural barriers to full participation in Canadian society.

Third, the government will promote creative encounters and interchange among all Canadian cultural groups in the interest of national unity.

Fourth, the government will continue to assist immigrants to acquire at least one of Canada's official languages in order to become full participants in Canadian society.[20]

Since 1971, the Government of Canada has consistently reinforced the policy of multiculturalism within a bilingual framework. First, there was the appointment of a minister of state responsible for multiculturalism in 1972, followed by the creation of a Multiculturalism Directorate in the Department of the Secretary of State. Then there was the passage of the Citizenship Act in 1977,[21] the Canadian Human Rights Act in 1977 which outlawed discrimination on grounds of race, national or ethnic origin, or colour,[22] and the Constitution Act of 1982 which entrenched both the individual and collective aspects of the policy of multiculturalism.[23] Finally, there was the Multicultural Act and the creation of a Ministry of Multicultualism in 1989.[24] In one form of another, all these measures have been designed to confirm English and French as the two official languages of Canada and the fact that Canada is composed of many diverse ethnic groups and communities, all of which have made significant contributions to Canadian development in general and Canadian cultural development in particular.

If the Royal Commission on Bilingualism and Biculturalism deserves to be considered a cultural landmark because it set in motion a chain of events which eventually led to Canada's current policy of multiculturalism within a bilingual framework, Expo and the Centennial celebrations deserve a similar commendation. Like the Royal Commission on Bilingualism and Biculturalism, these historic activities also set in motion a chain of events which has had a profound effect on Canada's cultural character over the last three decades. In fact, looking back, it is clear that Expo and the Centennial celebrations were responsible for ushering in a whole new era in Canadian cultural development.

CENTENNIAL TO THE PRESENT

Expo proved to be the perfect vehicle to open the doors on this new era. Taking place in Montreal in 1967, it exposed young and old alike to a vast panorama of possibilities, including, among countless other things, the artistic wizardry of the Czechs, the cultural achievements of the Asians, and the creative ingenuity of the Canadians in pavilions like Labyrinth and Man and His World.

If Expo was the jewel, the Centennial celebrations were the crown. For these were truly national celebrations. There was hardly a town, city or village in the country which did not seize the opportunity to create something of lasting value to commemorate Canada's one-hundredth birthday. Thanks to support provided by the federal government, the Centennial Commission, and provincial and municipal governments across the country, many communities built art galleries, museums, concert halls, theatres, auditoria, libraries, sports complexes and recreational centres in 1967, thereby laying the foundation for Canada's present system of cultural facilities. Moreover, hundreds of amateur, semi-professional and professional artists and arts organizations were provided with opportunities to perform and tour in different parts of the country.

For artists and arts organizations, Expo and the Centennial celebrations signalled the beginning of a new era in artistic development and maturity. For despite the fact that Canada's artists and arts organizations had been steadily sharpening their skills and expanding their repertoires for decades prior to 1967, no one was quite sure how these skills and repertoires would measure up to international scrutiny. Expo proved that Canada's artistic talents could take their rightful place alongside the best the world had to offer. This gave Canada's artistic community a confidence and maturity that was lacking before Expo but has never been lacking since. Such experiences confirmed the fact that the country's creative talents had a significant contribution to make to Canadian cultural development as well as to world cultural progress. Events of the last few decades have confirmed this fact, as Canadian artists and arts organizations have been accorded one international accolade after another in virtually every field of artistic endeavour.

For the public, Expo and the Centennial celebrations acted as a real watershed in public participation in the arts and culture. Prior to 1967, there was an elitist quality about the arts and arts audiences in Canada. Since 1967, the arts and arts audiences have been much more populist and broadly-based. The reason for this is not difficult to discern. People from many different socio-economic backgrounds and educational experiences had an opportunity to enjoy artistic and cultural activities as a result of Expo and the Centennial celebrations. This had the effect of dramatically increasing arts audiences, as well as extending them beyond the rich and the privileged.

For politicians and governments, Expo and the Centennial celebrations demonstrated that the arts and culture have a crucial role to play in Canada's municipal, provincial, national and international development. This awareness opened the doors to a new epoch in political understanding of the role of the arts and culture in the lives of Canadians and the country as a whole. It was no longer a question of whether governments should be involved in Canadian cultural development, but rather what form this involvement should take.

The federal government was quick to capitalize on the success of Expo and the Centennial celebrations. In the period between 1967 and 1972, it initiated a number of fundamental improvements in Canada's cultural system. It is one of the few times the federal government — and indeed any government in Canada, with the possible exception of Quebec — has acted in a proactive rather than reactive manner. In the space of a few short years, it passed a Broadcasting Act, created the Canadian Radio-Television Commission (now the Canadian Radio-Television and Telecommunications Commission), established the National Museums Corporation, set up the Canadian Film Development Corporation (now Telefilm Canada) and completed the National Arts Centre. It also set out the guidelines for a national cultural policy. Little wonder this period from 1967 to 1972 is recognized as one of the most fertile periods in Canadian cultural history.

Many preparatory developments were necessary to make these federal initiatives a reality. Most of these developments took place in the period immediately leading up to Expo and the Centennial celebrations. Foremost among the developments were: reorganization of the Department of the Secretary of State in 1963 mentioned earlier; and creation of a Cultural Affairs Division in the Department of External Affairs in 1966 (now the Department of Foreign Affairs and International Trade). If Canada was to celebrate one hundred years of Confederation and make its mark on the international scene, an infrastructure was required at the federal level equal to the challenge. By reorganizing the Department of Secretary of State and creating a Cultural Affairs Division in the Department of External Affairs, the federal government was giving official recognition to the fact that culture had a key role to play in the country's domestic and international development in the future.

With these bureaucratic and structural requirements in place, the federal government was in a perfect position to pass the **Broadcasting Act** of 1968. In order to ensure that the country's rapidly-evolving broadcasting system was operated in the national interest and capable of coping with pressures from American broadcasters, the Act stipulated that:

> the Canadian broadcasting system should be effectively owned and controlled by Canadians so as to safeguard, enrich and strengthen the cultural, political, social and economic fabric of Canada.[25]

In order to reinforce the country's bilingual nature and assert the need for national unity and identity, the Act when on to stipulate that:

> all Canadians are entitled to broadcasting service in English and French as public funds become available (and)...the national broadcasting service should contribute to the development of national unity and provide for a continuing expression of Canadian identity.[26]

This is the first time an **official** link was stated between Canadian cultural policy and national unity by the federal government.[27] The country's artists and arts organizations had paved the way for this when they made their presentation to the Turgeon Committee on Reconstruction and Re-establishment in 1944. It was reinforced by the Massey-Lévesque Commission in 1951, when it asserted the role that art, education and culture are capable of playing in keeping the country together and assuring Canadian unity and identity.

In order to ensure that the sentiments and objectives of the Broadcasting Act were adhered to in practice, the federal government established the Canadian Radio-Television Commission in 1968 to regulate the broadcasting system in the national interest. The impact of the Commission was felt almost immediately. Under the leadership of Pierre Juneau and the introduction of some tough regulatory measures, the CRTC was instrumental in instituting a number of key changes in public and private broadcasting, particularly in the area of broadcast licensing and Canadian content. These changes were mirrored in the area of film when the Canadian Film Development Corporation was created in 1968 to provide assistance to Canadian film-makers and film houses through a variety of subsidy measures, capital cost allowances and incentives to show Canadian films.

With all this activity taking place, it was apparent that the country needed a national cultural policy. Not coincidentally, recognition of this need came at the same time that pressure was building internationally to formulate cultural policies. This pressure was being exerted by UNESCO (United Nations Educational, Scientific and Cultural Organization). In many ways, it had been created precisely for this purpose. Between 1967 and 1970, it laid the groundwork for the first World Conference on Cultural Policies which was held in Venice in 1970.[28] This enchanting place proved to be the ideal location for one of the greatest international landmarks in cultural history. For the first time in history, ministers with responsibility for culture from over one hundred countries in the world met to consider a variety of issues related to cultural development and policy and the role of government in cultural life.

In Canada, responsibility for preparation for the first World Conference on Cultural Policies, and more generally development of a national cultural policy, fell to Gérard Pelletier. He proved to be the ideal person to assume these tasks. Not only did he have extensive experience in culture, politics, the media and international affairs, but also he had taken over from Judy LaMarsh as Secretary of State in 1968 and was a close friend of Prime Minister Trudeau.

No sooner was Pelletier in office than he turned his attention to the development of a cultural policy for Canada. In a speech to the Montreal Board of Trade in October 1968 titled **Towards the Definition of a Cultural Policy (Vers la definition d'une politique culturelle)**, Pelletier indicated how essential he felt it was for Canada to have a dynamic and coherent national cultural policy. At the First National Forum on Cultural Policy, organized by the Canadian Conference of the Arts in Toronto in 1970, Pelletier set out what he believed to be the general guidelines for such a policy. These he identified as: pluralism; democratization; decentralization; federal-provincial relations; and international co-operation. The objectives behind these guidelines were clear. They were to make the country's proliferating collection of cultural assets accessible to all Canadians, regardless of age, gender, economic status, religious affiliation, educational level, ethnic background or geographical location.

While all the guidelines related to the connection between culture and politics in one form or another, clearly the guidelines concerning pluralism, democratization and decentralization were most significant. The guideline respecting pluralism was designed to reinforce the Government's commitment to multiculturalism within a bilingual framework, thereby opening the doors to the variety of multicultural initiatives and activities mentioned earlier. The guidelines respecting democratization and decentralization were designed to counteract elitism and centralism in Canadian cultural life. Not only were they intended to open up cultural institutions and activities to all Canadians, but also they were intended to increase citizen participation in cultural life. Interestingly, commitment to the "twin engines" of democratization and decentralization was not unique to Canada. It was evident in many countries throughout the world, particularly countries like France which were anxious to broaden and deepen citizen involvement in cultural life and break the tendency for artists and artists organizations to accumulate in major urban centres like Paris. Clearly governments could only justify the use of public funds to support cultural activities if a much larger and more representative segment of the population was involved in these activities.

Having set out the guidelines for a national cultural policy for Canada, Pelletier and officials in the Department of the Secretary of State turned their attention to the development of policies for three specific sectors of Canadian cultural life. Between 1970 and 1973, they launched policies for film, publishing, and museums.[29] Not surprisingly, concern for democratization and decentralization figured prominently in these policies. In publishing, for example, emphasis was placed on increasing the production and distribution of books in Canada through a variety of measures including grants to publishers, purchase of Canadian books, assistance for translations, and representations at international book fairs. In film, film production and distribution were promoted through more effective use of Canadian films by cultural agencies in general and the CBC in particular, creation of regional centres for the NFB, and more financial assistance for the Canadian Film Development Corporation. For museums, the policy encompassed a programme of associate museums to the national museums in Ottawa, exhibition centres in remote areas, the use of museummoblies, creation of a Canadian Conservation Institute and a Canadian Heritage Information Network, and strengthening of the National Museums Corporation to co-ordinate the work of all federal museums. As these policies indicate, the federal government could act with considerable force and conviction when it tackled cultural issues and problems consistent with its own political interests and aspirations. Moreover, it had many tools and techniques at its disposal to accomplish the objectives at hand, including grants, subsidies, programmes, purchases, legislation, regulation, research, information, statistics, creation of cultural agencies, and a variety of tax measures.

It was not long before concern for democratization and decentralization started to manifest itself in the practices of the federal cultural agencies, even though these agencies had a great deal of autonomy and control over their own affairs. For example, democratization and decentralization provided the impetus behind the Canada Council's Art Bank, Touring Office and Exploration programme, which were all launched immediately after the release of the publishing, film and museums policies. These programmes were financed through special funds provided by the Department of the Secretary of State and were designed to move the arts out of their traditional locations in art galleries, museums, theatres and concert halls and expose them to a broader cross-section of the Canadian population. Democratization and decentralization also figured prominently in the programmes and activities of the National Museums Corporation. Following reorganization of the National Museum of Science, the National Museum of Technology, the National Museum of Natural Sciences, the National Museum of Man and the National Gallery of Art under the National Museums Corporation in 1968, the country's national museums were in an ideal position to make the country's rapidly-escalating heritage accessible to more Canadians. This was accomplished through a variety of measures designed to assist museums and art galleries throughout the country to up-grade their services, expand their facilities, improve their educational, training and extension programmes, and move their artefacts and collections to more remote parts of the country.

There is one final federal government initiative which should be mentioned here because it was destined to have an important impact on the cultural life of the country in the decades to follow.

When Opportunities for Youth (OFY) and the Local Initiatives Program (LIP) were created in the early 1970s, few expected them to have a cultural impact on the country. After all, they were designed to combat tardy rates of economic growth, recessionary conditions and high levels of unemployment, particularly among young people and seasonal workers. Nevertheless, by providing opportunities for people to create employment activities of their own choosing, OFY and LIP opened the doors to a cornucopia of possibilities. Although the estimates vary considerably depending on how "art" and "culture" are defined, there is a consensus that the number of arts and cultural projects undertaken through these highly innovative programmes was exceedingly high — anywhere from twenty to sixty percent depending on the definitions used. In retrospect, the reason for this is clear. The demand for artistic and cultural resources was running well ahead of the supply in all parts of the country. As a result, a new wave of artistic and cultural organizations made their appearance on the scene, typified by such organizations as Vancouver's East Cultural Centre, Toronto's Factory Lab and Tarragon theatres, and Newfoundland's Mummers Theatre. Not only did these and other organizations initiated as a result of OFY and LIP become permanent fixtures on the Canadian cultural scene, but also they were heavily committed to reaching new audiences and creating Canadian works. They came just in time. For tensions and frustrations were building rapidly in the arts community with respect to the adverse socio-economic condition of artists and arts organizations, lack of Canadian content, and too much reliance on European and especially American programming.

Many of these tensions and frustrations were vented during the **Direction Canada** consultations which were held in 1972 and 1973 with more than a thousand of the country's artists and members of the cultural community. Organized by the Canadian Conference of the Arts, these consultations involved regional meetings in different parts of the country and culminated with a national meeting in Ottawa. When the more than 2,000 recommendations emanating from these consultations were classified according to area of concern and frequency with which the concern was expressed, they provided a valuable list of the most pressing concerns confronting Canadian artists, arts administrators and arts organizations at that time. In descending order of importance, these concerns were: improve the status of Canadian artists; increase funding for the arts; decentralize cultural activity and policy; improve arts education; democratize access to the arts; distribute more information on Canadian and international activities; increase media support for cultural development; and improve the administration of cultural resources.[30] As this list demonstrated only too well, not only were democratization and decentralization among the key concerns of the cultural community, but also much more progress was required to improve the social-economic condition of artists and arts organizations. For despite the progress which had been recorded in the cultural field since the end of World War II, **Direction Canada** revealed that the country's artists and arts organizations were still required to carry the bulk of the burden of Canada's cultural development through low wages, high unemployment, lack of social security benefits and poor working conditions.

While these developments were taking place at the regional and national level, important developments were taking place at the provincial level. Between 1970 and 1980, many provincial governments set up departments or ministries of culture to complement the arts councils, branches of government departments, and support mechanisms they had established earlier. The objective was not only to expand provincial involvement in cultural development, but also to consolidate many diverse activities under one roof, such as the arts, crafts, sports, recreation, communications, heritage and citizenship.

Quebec was once again at the forefront of these developments. Not only was the Ministère des Affairs culturelles reorganized and expanded, but in 1976 it released the first comprehensive governmental report on cultural policy in Canada. Entitled **Towards the Evolution of a Cultural Policy (Pour l'évolution de la politique culturelle)**, it called for a greatly expanded role for the arts and culture in Quebec's future development. In 1977, Bill 101 was passed describing the regulations governing language in Quebec and strengthening the intimate bond between language and culture. In addition, the government created a super-ministry of state for cultural development and appointed Camille Laurin as the Minister of State for Cultural Development. He promptly sanctioned the creation of regional cultural councils throughout Quebec to advise the Government and the Ministry on cultural matters. Moreover, he sanctioned preparation of another major position paper on culture. Entitled **A Cultural Development Policy for Quebec (La politique québécoise du développement culturel)**,[31] it took a significantly broader view of culture in general and Quebec culture in particular. It was a view which included education, the environment, science, architecture, food and dress as well as the arts, heritage and language in culture. This was confirmed by the paper's author, Fernand

Dumont, when he said: "I have always considered a collective project as something mainly cultural. The economy is not an end in itself: culture is."[32] Not surprisingly, the paper commenced as follows:

> More and more countries are today beginning to rethink their cultural programs, and to draw up policies encompassing the whole of their culture. Québec too is involved in this process. [33]

Cast in these terms, the paper foreshadowed some of the developments taking place in the cultural field today, particularly the trend towards a more comprehensive understanding of culture.[34] As such, it may prove to be a forerunner for some of the changes which will be needed in the cultural and political fields in Canada in the future.

While the Quebec government was moving faster and farther in its quest to recognize the key role that culture plays in the lives of people and the affairs of societies, it was not the only provincial government to be initiating developments on this front. In Alberta, Ontario, Saskatchewan and Nova Scotia, Alberta Culture, Ontario's Ministry of Culture and Recreation, Saskatchewan's Ministry of Culture and Youth, and Nova Scotia's Department of Recreation were all established during the period between 1970 and 1980. By 1980, every province in the country had at least one, and in some cases two, administrative institutions to advance the cultural cause and promote cultural development. While the same claim could not be made for municipalities — except for Vancouver, Calgary, Toronto and Montreal where an arts council, a government department, or both, existed to advance cultural interests — there was nevertheless a significant increase in municipal cultural funding during this period.[35] This served to demonstrate the growing importance the country's municipalities were attaching to culture, as well as an indication that better things were on their way at the local level.

All this activity in the public sector was matched by activity in the private sector. In response to the escalating demand for artistic activities, the nation's artists and arts organizations were busy fashioning the plays, paintings, novels, stories, poems and concerts which were needed to satisfy this demand. As a result, the country's theatres, concert halls, arts centres, galleries and museums were pressed into active service. In addition, many new cultural facilities were created during this period, thanks to funding programmes like Wintario and the Capital Grants Program of the Department of the Secretary of State. The latter programme was particularly helpful in preserving some of the country's century-old theatres, opera houses and concert halls from demolition and converting them to modern use.

With this expansion in the cultural life and facilities of the country came empirical evidence that the arts and culture were making a significant contribution to the Canadian economy. In places like Stratford, Niagara-on-the-Lake and Lennoxville, detailed studies were conducted to prove that this contribution was not limited to purchases of tickets for events, but also included expenditures on hotels, motels, meals, transportation, merchandise, and the attraction of business and industry.[36] These same benefits were being experienced in cities like Vancouver, Calgary, Winnipeg, Toronto, Montreal, Halifax and Saint John's, although it was difficult to ascertain the exact size of these contributions due to a variety of methodological problems related to isolating economic and cultural factors in large urban environments.

It was within this overall climate of rapid growth and increased public involvement in the cultural life of the country that pressure was building to undertake a second Massey-Lévesque Commission. Three decades had elapsed since the Commission concluded its work and many in the cultural community felt the situation was so changed that another major assessment was needed of the country's cultural needs and future directions.

The Conservative Government responded to this pressure after it assumed power in 1979 by establishing the Federal Cultural Policy Review Committee. It provided it with a mandate to evaluate the principles, policies and practices on which Canada's cultural development should be based and make recommendations concerning its future development. While the Committee did not have the status of a Royal Commission, it had a large budget and the freedom to probe deeply into the cultural life of the country.

In the execution of its work, the Committee was immediately confronted with a whole series of complex procedural issues and problems — issues and problems which simply did not exist when the Massey-Lévesque Commission conducted its work because the cultural infrastructure of the country was far less complicated at that time. For example, what role should government in general — and federal, provincial and municipal governments in particular — play in the country's cultural development? Should the federal government establish a ministry of culture, or were autonomous cultural agencies and a government department which included other responsibilities sufficient? What relationship should exist between the Department of Communication, which by this time had taken over from the Department of the Secretary of State as the key cultural department in government, and the Canada Council, the CBC, the NFB, the National Museums Corporation and the National Arts Centre? How could accountability be assured when so many decisions respecting the use of tax-payers funds were made by cultural agencies at arm's length from government and the political process? While many believed the Committee should have taken a more visionary approach to its work, it is clear in retrospect why the Committee zeroed in on procedural issues and problems. Given the bureaucratic changes that had taken place since the Massey-Lévesque Commission and the fact that many more cultural departments and agencies were engaged in cultural development, numerous procedural issues and problems had to be sorted out if Canadian cultural development was to thrive in the years and decades ahead.

In the process of addressing these issues and problems, the Federal Cultural Policy Review Committee came down strongly on the side of the arm's length principle and maintaining a healthy distance between politics, government and culture.[37] It recommended passage of a Cultural Agencies Act to ensure the necessary independence of the arts and culture from government, particularly in areas affecting the allocation of public funds for cultural purposes.

While little controversy surrounded the Committee's recommendations concerning the arts and the arm's length principle, a heated debate erupted over the Committee's recommendations concerning the CBC and NFB. This tended to overshadow many of the valuable recommendations the Committee made with respect to the development and administration of artistic activities in Canada. For despite the fact that the Committee argued vigorously for adherence to artistic rather than political or economic objectives and creation of several new cultural agencies, including a Canadian Heritage Council and a Canadian International Cultural Relations Agency, the press, the public, and the profession seized on the Committee's recommendations concerning the "privatization" and "downsizing" of the CBC and the NFB. Although the Committee felt that the private sector had grown to the point where it was better for the CBC and NFB to utilize private-sector resources than produce programmes in house, it probably under-estimated the extent to which the CBC and NFB had become "cultural icons" in Canada. While the Committee's recommendations concerning the CBC and NFB were not shared by the cultural community, the media or the public, they did send out a strong signal that much more emphasis was going to be placed on the private sector and the marketplace in the future. Not only was this consistent with the shift that was taking place from a liberal to a conservative political ideology, but also it was clear that the days of substantial increases in public funding for the arts and culture were coming to an end.

It did not take the cultural community long to get the message. Throughout the 1980s, the community focused on developing private sector sources of support, as well as on marketing, management, fund-raising and board development. While attempts were made to lobby federal, provincial and municipal governments for more support, there was a growing realization that more funds would have to come from box office sources, admissions, sponsorships, special events, sale of products, audience development and monies raised from corporations, foundations and private benefactors.

Meanwhile, a number of developments on the international front was having an impact on cultural policies and practices in Canada. For example, UNESCO convened the second World Conference on Cultural Policies in Mexico City in 1982, following regional cultural policy conferences for Europe, Africa, Asia and Latin America in the 1970s. This had the effect of increasing interest in cultural policies in Canada, as well as focusing attention on the pivotal role governments play in cultural development. It also had the effect of broadening understanding of the nature, meaning and scope of culture. Prior to the Mexico City Conference, culture was defined by UNESCO largely in terms of the arts, heritage and cultural industries of publishing, radio, television, film and video. At Mexico City, UNESCO defined culture in significantly broader terms as "the whole collection of distinctive traits, spiritual and material, intellectual and affective, which characterize a society or social group. It comprises, besides arts and letters, modes of life, human rights, value systems, traditions and beliefs."[38] Given the fact that this much more comprehensive definition of culture was endorsed by all member states of UNESCO including Canada, it was bound to have a bearing on perceptions of culture everywhere in the world.

A number of developments taking place in Canada corresponded to these international developments, particularly concerning the formulation and implementation of cultural policies. For example, the federal government announced a new national broadcasting policy in 1983. It was designed to enrich Canadian programming through the creation of a Canadian Broadcast Program Development Fund, as well as to assert the importance of the CBC in the overall broadcasting system. The federal government also announced policies for film and video at this time to ensure the economic viability of private-sector film and video production in Canada. These policies were reflective of the growing interest in the cultural industries in Canada and other parts of the world, as well as the desire to include the cultural industries in political definitions of culture.[39] They were also reflective of structural changes taking place within the federal government. In the early 1980s, the Arts and Culture Branch of the Department of the Secretary of State was transferred to the Department of Communication. This was consistent with the view that "cultural hardware" and "cultural software" should be housed under the same departmental roof. It was also consistent with the view that communications and technology had so transformed cultural life in Canada that new approaches were needed to come to grips with them. At least that was the opinion of Marcel Masse, who was appointed Minister of Communications in 1984. No sooner was Masse in office than he sanctioned a number of major policy studies for broadcasting, film, museums, funding, the National Arts Centre and the Status of the Artist.[40] It was clear by this time that the conservative political ideology was having a fundamental impact on cultural policies and practices in Canada.

At the provincial level, many provincial governments seized the opportunity to introduce policy changes of their own. Consistent with changes at the federal level, many of these changes centred on the need to articulate more effective cultural policies, improve administrative structures, enhance delivery systems, and deal more effectively with the cultural industries. For example, Nova Scotia and Ontario conducted major policy studies and issued important cultural policy statements, thereby complementing policy statements released earlier by Alberta and Manitoba. Most of these statements came down strongly on the side of the arm's length principle and maintaining a healthy distance between politics and culture. In Quebec, where cultural matters were being pursued more vigorously than elsewhere in the country, policy statements were issued for dance and theatre in 1984. Moreover, in 1987, the Quebec Government passed legislation on the status of the artist — the first significant legislation on this subject to be passed by any government in Canada. The benefits of this legislation became apparent in 1988 when Quebec's Minister of Revenue granted artists the status of "self-employed workers," thereby allowing them to claim certain work-related expenses as income tax deductions. This step was capped at the end of the decade by a substantial increase in the budget of the Ministère des Affaires culturelles.

These developments at the provincial and national levels did not go unnoticed at the municipal level. Although municipal governments were less involved in cultural matters than their federal and provincial counterparts, many municipalities were interested in becoming more involved in the cultural life of the country. Their interest centred on the need to up-grade services, articulate policies, improve administrative structures, and increase funding. As a result, many municipal governments expanded their cultural programmes, adopted arts and cultural policies, consolidated their infrastructure and increased funding in the decade between 1980 and 1990. By the end of the decade, governments at all levels were playing an active role in cultural development in Canada.

It is impossible to complete this examination of the past without mentioning two final developments which have had a profound effect on culture and politics and the relationship between them in the 1980s and 1990s. The first is the crisis of national unity and the difficulties between Quebec and the rest of Canada. The second is the free trade movement and the signing of the North American Free Trade Agreement.

Reference was made earlier to developments in the 1960s, 1970s and 1980s with respect to bilingualism, biculturalism and multiculturalism, including the Royal Commission on Bilingualism and Biculturalism, the endorsement of the official policy of multiculturalism within a bilingual framework, the passage of the Official Languages Act, and the creation of a federal Ministry of Multiculturalism. While these developments were generally accepted throughout the country, they were viewed differently in Quebec. There, along with other factors, they contributed to the growing sense of frustration and alienation, as well as the movement towards separatism.

The federal government responded to this situation by establishing the Task Force on National Unity in 1979 under the joint chairmanship of Jean-Luc Pepin and John Robarts. While the Task Force made many valuable recommendations concerning national unity and identity, especially in the areas of federal-provincial relations, distribution of federal-provincial powers and recognition of the crucial importance of language and culture in Canadian development,[41] these recommendations did not have a fundamental impact on the Quebec situation or relations between Quebec and the rest of Canada. This problem was exacerbated when the federal government and every province except Quebec reached an agreement on a method for patriating the Canadian Constitution in 1981. It was aggravated even more when the Constitution was patriated in 1982 without the approval of Quebec.

When the Conservative Government came to power in 1984, it proposed dealing with this situation by amending the Constitution Act of 1982 to "bring Quebec into the constitutional family." This led to the Meech Lake Accord of 1987, which was agreed to **in principle** by the federal government and all provincial governments including Quebec. As the time drew near to ratify the Accord, however, support for it had waned, largely because provincial governments had changed since the Accord was originally formulated. When Manitoba failed to ratify the Accord in their legislature and Newfoundland withdrew support for it, the Accord died in 1990. This resulted in a number of federal-provincial conferences, as well as a variety of efforts to create a new agreement which would recognize

Quebec's cultural, linguistic and legal distinctiveness. This led to the creation of a new federal-provincial agreement in 1992 — the Charlottetown Accord. It was designed to recognize Quebec's distinct language and culture and transfer authority over mining, forestry, telecommunications and other jurisdictions to the provinces. When a national referendum was held on the Charlottetown Accord in 1992, however, it was rejected by a small majority of Canadians. By this time, the Liberals had replaced the Conservatives at the federal level. They were taken aback when a referendum on separation in Quebec in 1995 was defeated by the narrowest of margins. This put Quebec and the rest of Canada on a collision course. The provincial governments attempted to alter this course in 1997 by convening a major conference on national unity. While Quebec and the federal government were not present at the conference, the conference did produce a number of proposals designed to recognize the uniqueness of Quebec, confirm the equality of all provinces and people of Canada, and initiate a "bottom-up" approach to constitutional change and national unity.

The other significant development affecting culture and politics and the complex connection between them in the 1980s and 1990s was the free trade movement and the signing of the North American Free Trade Agreement.

Developments on this front can be traced back to 1987 when the Conservative Government decided to pursue an international policy based on free trade rather than protection. This resulted in the signing of the Canada-United States Free Trade Agreement. It called for the elimination of all cross-border tariffs within a ten year period. While the Agreement was originally rejected by both opposition parties and the Senate, it was approved in 1989 after the Conservative Government won a majority in 1988. This opened the doors for a much broader free trade agreement involving Canada, the United States and Mexico. It resulted in the North American Free Trade Agreement (NAFTA) of 1992.

Since that time, Canada, United States and Mexico have moved closer together. Not only have exports and imports increased significantly among the three countries, but also substantial capital and industrial movements have taken place as corporations and companies search for the best locations for their economic and commercial operations. By 1997, the North American Free Trade Agreement and the crisis of national unity were having a profound effect on individuals and institutions in all parts of the country. Together with the deficit and debt situation, corporate and government downsizing and cost-cutting, high unemployment and the shift from a liberal to a conservative political ideology, they were transforming cultural and political life in every region and province of the country.

This completes the historical examination of culture and politics and the complex connection between them. Looking back, what conclusions can be drawn and observations made which are helpful in shedding light on the present situation and preparations for the future?

CONCLUSIONS AND OBSERVATIONS

An initial conclusion is obvious. Both the cultural and political fields have grown substantially over the last three or four centuries and particularly over the last fifty years. Not only has there been a substantial increase in the number of artists, arts, media and heritage organizations, cultural agencies and cultural associations, but also there has been a phenomenal increase in the size of governments, government departments, programmes, policies and legislative enactments. Superimposed on this pattern of general growth are a number of specific institutions, events and activities which has had a particularly powerful effect on the cultural life of the country. Included among these institutions, events and activities are the Canadian Broadcasting Corporation, the National Film Board, the Canada Council for the Arts, the Canadian Radio-Television and Telecommunications Commission, the Massey-Lévesque Commission, Expo and the Centennial celebrations, the Royal Commission on

Bilingualism and Biculturalism, and others. Political authorities have also played an important role, particularly authorities like Wilfrid Laurier, Mackenzie King, the Earl of Dufferin, the Marquis of Lorne, Lord Bessborough, Vincent Massey, Georges-Henri Lévesque, Pierre Trudeau, Maurice Lamontagne, Judy LaMarsh, Gérard Pelletier, Camille Laurin, and others. Combined with the general growth that has taken place, these institutions, events, activities and political personalities have contributed to the high level of cultural development in Canada today.

A second conclusion is equally obvious. As the political and cultural fields have grown, so has the relationship between them. At the time of Confederation, culture and politics were largely separate fields of activity. Today, there is an intimate connection between them. This is apparent as soon as consideration is given to the many issues with political and cultural implications confronting the country and its citizenry today, including unity, identity, free trade, bilingualism, multiculturalism, regionalism, and relations between Quebec and the rest of Canada. There have been times when governments have played a proactive role in addressing these issues. The most conspicuous example of this is Expo, the Centennial celebrations, and the flurry of governmental activity and legislation which took place immediately following this historic occasion. More often than not, however, governments have played a reactive role. This is consistent with a responsive theory of government and the belief that the impetus for change should come from citizens and community groups rather than from governments in a democratic society. Nevertheless, it does raise a moot point. Can the host of issues with cultural and political implications confronting Canada and Canadians today be resolved without a proactive approach on the part of the country's governments?

A third conclusion is also apparent. As the connection between culture and politics has broadened and deepened, governments at all levels have been compelled to confront a whole series of complex and difficult cultural problems. Most of these problems relate to how to "operationalize" culture in government and the political process.

Governments have sought solutions to this challenge largely by drawing on practices and policies prevalent elsewhere. This has had both a positive and negative effect on cultural development in Canada. On the positive side, it has yielded tailor-made solutions to some of the country's most difficult and demanding cultural challenges, especially developing suitable operational definitions of culture and Canadian culture, evolving effective models of cultural development, working out acceptable techniques for developing the cultural sector, establishing measures to protect culture from too much political interference, and designing successful methods for allocating financial assistance to the arts, artists, arts organizations and the cultural industries. On the negative side, it has meant that indigenous solutions have not been forthcoming to some of Canada's most deep-seated cultural problems and culture has been marginalized in government because it has been defined in very narrow terms. One consequence of this is that issues like national unity and identity, Canadian content, the Americanization of Canadian culture, and the role of the country's artists and arts and media organizations in Canadian development have not received the attention and priority they need in government affairs and the political process. Whether this will suffice in the future is a debatable point, given the Quebec situation, the constitutional crisis, the difficulties related to national unity and identity, the threat of American domination of Canadian culture, and the erosion of many Canadian values and traditions. Perhaps the time has come to search for solutions to the country's political and cultural problems which are more finely tuned to the country's own historical reality, indigenous requirements and future needs.

A final conclusion is also evident. As culture and politics have moved closer together, culture has become steadily more politicized in Canada. For the cultural community, this has meant greater involvement in political affairs, as well as much more lobbying and advocacy. For governments, it has meant careful evaluation of cultural commitments, priorities and policies. This is imperative in view of the present political and cultural realities confronting Canada and Canadians today. It is to this situation that attention can now be directed.

THE REALITY OF THE PRESENT

> The essential problem to be tackled by any federal
> cultural policy in Canada is how to make it possible
> for Canadians to create, distribute, use and enjoy
> Canadian materials of all kinds. [1]
>
> Jack Gray

Due to the rapid growth of the cultural field over the last few centuries and particularly over the last fifty years, the simplicity of earlier decades and centuries has disappeared. Culture is big business in Canada today. Not only does it make a significant contribution to the Canadian economy, but also it is intricately interwoven into the political process. As a result, there could be no better time to undertake an examination of the present state of Canadian culture and the country's cultural sector.

SIGNIFICANCE OF THE CULTURAL SECTOR

When Canadian culture is defined in terms of the arts, heritage and cultural industries — that is to say the way most governments define the country's culture today — Canada's cultural sector is substantial in size, dynamic in character and complex in nature. Subdivided into large public and private components, the cultural sector has a labour force of approximately 650,000 to 700,000 workers and makes an annual contribution to the Canadian economy of roughly 20 to 25 billion dollars depending on what is included and excluded from the definition of the arts, heritage and cultural industries. [2] Clearly the cultural sector stands alongside other major sectors of economic activity in Canada.

The private component of the cultural sector consists of a number of different networks. First, there is the network of artists, arts and heritage organizations, and special events. It consists of all the visual artists, poets, playwrights, composers, musicians, actors, actresses, managers, administrators, orchestras, choirs, theatre and dance companies, art galleries, museums and festivals which exist throughout the country. These individuals, institutions and events exist at every level of activity — from fledgling amateur and non-profit to fully professional and commercial — as well as in every urban, suburban and rural setting across the country.

Joining this network of artists, arts and heritage organizations and special events are other networks designed to serve more specific functions. First of all, there is the cultural industries' network. It consists of all the publishing houses, radio and television stations, film companies, recording studios and craft associations that exist across the country. It is concerned with the production, distribution and consumption of cultural works in material or media rather than live form. Then there is the facilities' network. It consists of all the theatres, concert halls, arts centres and the like from coast to coast. After this comes the service and professional associations' network. At the national level alone, it numbers more than a hundred organizations. To this must be added the thousands of provincial and municipal associations and community arts councils which exist across the country. Then there is the educational network. It consists of all the courses and programmes in the arts and culture which are offered at elementary and secondary schools, community colleges, universities, and special institutions like the National Theatre School, the National Ballet School, the Banff Centre, and others. This network is concerned with providing opportunities to Canadians to learn about the arts and culture in the educational system. Finally, there are the funding and voluntary networks. The funding network consists of all the corporations, foundations and private patrons providing financial assistance to the arts and culture in Canada. The voluntary network consists of all the people sitting on the boards of arts and cultural organizations and providing a variety of other services to these organizations.

These networks play an indispensable role in providing the thousands of artistic and cultural performances, exhibitions, programmes and courses which Canadians enjoy each year. Although there are considerable variations depending on the types of activities provided and their geographical location across the country, the overall picture which emerges is one of substantial citizen involvement in the cultural life of the country through attendance at concerts and plays, visits to art galleries and museums, enrolment in arts courses, and appreciation of cultural activities in the media.[3]

The public component of the cultural sector is equally substantial in size and complex in nature. It consists of all the government departments, branches of government departments and specialized agencies involved in cultural development in Canada, from conservation, preservation, creation and distribution to planning, programming, funding, policy development, fiscal management, administration and regulation.

At the federal level, this involvement cuts across virtually every department of government, from Canadian Heritage, Foreign Affairs and International Trade and the Secretary of State to Human Resources Development, Citizenship and Immigration, Public Works, Revenue Canada, Statistics Canada and Environment Canada. The pervasiveness of the federal government in the cultural development of the country is felt not only through these and other government departments, but also through numerous cultural agencies, such as the Canadian Broadcasting Corporation, Canada Council for the Arts, National Gallery of Canada, National Museum of Science and Technology, National Museum of Natural History, Canadian Museum of Civilization, National Film Board, Telefilm Canada, National Arts Centre, National Library, Public Archives, Historic Sites and Monuments Board, Canadian Radio-Television and Telecommunications Commission, and others This same pattern of government involvement is evident at the provincial and municipal levels, despite the fact that there are substantial variations from region to region, province to province and municipality to municipality.

A cultural sector of this size and significance is bound to be confronted with numerous difficulties. In recent years, many of these difficulties emanate from the fact that governments in all parts of the country have been forced to cope with some exceedingly difficult financial problems. While some governments have been able to address these problems more effectively than others, there is hardly a government anywhere in the country which is not wrestling with debts, deficits, cost-cutting, downsizing, and the redistribution of federal-provincial-municipal powers. This is coming at a time when the country is experiencing high levels of unemployment, a great deal of labour-management unrest, pressure to preserve health care, social and educational programmes, and numerous environmental requirements. These problems are having a profound effect on the country's cultural sector, as recent cuts in government spending on culture in general, and cuts to the Department of Canadian Heritage, the Canadian Broadcasting Corporation, the Canada Council for the Arts, and many provincial and municipal cultural departments and agencies across the country, confirm.[4] Not only does this intensify the trend towards greater politicization of culture, but also it makes it more essential than ever to broaden and deepen understanding of the complex connection between culture and politics.

ADMINISTRATION OF THE CULTURAL SECTOR

Over the centuries, Canada has evolved an unique administrative structure to govern its cultural development. It is a structure which reflects the division of the cultural sector into large public and private components.

The private component is administered by individuals and institutions outside government. These individuals and institutions possess a high degree of authority and autonomy over their own affairs, although many are dependent on funds from governments, corporations, foundations and wealthy benefactors. This contrasts with many European countries, where the State often plays a more direct and active role in the ownership, control, financing or operation of opera and ballet companies, symphony orchestras, theatre companies, art galleries and museums.

The public component of the cultural sector is administered by government cultural departments and cultural agencies situated at arm's length from government and the political process. This component is a hybrid of the French and British models of cultural development. On the one hand, there is the French model, where government cultural departments play an active and direct role. On the other hand, there is the British model, where arts councils and other types of autonomous agencies play a key role. For the French, there appears to be no need to have a buffer between government, the cultural community and the general public: governments and government cultural departments usually play a straight-forward and highly-participatory role. For the British, there appears to be every reason to have a buffer between government, the cultural community and the general public.

As the inheritor of this dualistic approach to public cultural administration, Canada has evolved a system of cultural administration over the last century, and particularly over the last fifty years, which usually includes both a government department and an arm's length cultural agency working at the same jurisdictional level. Take funding as one illustration of this. At the federal level, there is the Department of Canadian Heritage, which operates very much like a department of culture except in name, and the Canada Council for the Arts. At the provincial level, there is the Ministry of Citizenship, Culture and Recreation and the Ontario Arts Council in Ontario, the Ministère de la Culture et des Communications du Québec and the Conseil des Arts du Québec in Quebec, the Department of Tourism, Culture and Recreation and the Newfoundland and Labrador Arts Council in Newfoundland, and the Ministry of Small Business, Tourism and Culture and the British Columbia Arts Council in British Columbia. Most other provinces also have a department of government and an arts council or its equivalent providing funding for the arts, even if there have been many changes in this pattern in recent years. The same pattern is often repeated at the municipal level. Many municipalities have a government department — often a department of parks, recreation and culture — and an arts council engaged in funding artistic activities.

Although it is seldom recognized in Canada, this hybrid system is the envy of virtually every country in the world. The reason for this is apparent. There is political clout and direct representation in government through departments of culture, as well as autonomy and freedom of expression through arts councils operating at arm's length from government and the political process. Countries without departments of culture bemoan the fact that there is insufficient representation in government to produce the necessary financial, capital and human resources. Countries without arts councils bemoan the fact that there is too little freedom from government and too much political interference in decisions affecting cultural life.

Although this system is not without its problems, especially in the area of duplication of services and confusion over the roles and responsibilities of government departments and arm's length arts councils, no greater mistake could be made than to assume that the country should have either departments of culture **or** arts councils. The historical evolution of culture in Canada has produced a situation where the country has both. Moreover, the country needs both. It needs strong departments of culture capable of addressing cultural problems head on in government and the political process. However, it also needs strong arts councils capable of preserving freedom and preventing too much political interference in cultural affairs. While every effort should be made to clarify areas of responsibility and eliminate duplication whenever and wherever it is encountered, the country would be well advised to maintain its unique administrative system for cultural development. This means working to ensure that effective relationships are maintained between government cultural departments, arts councils and other types of cultural agencies. This is imperative in a country where the cultural sector has a crucial role to play in national unity, identity, survival and development.

PRINCIPLES OF CULTURAL ADMINISTRATION

If Canada possesses a system of public cultural administration which is unique, it also possesses a system which is predicated on a number of basic principles. These principles — commitment to excellence, creativity, freedom, access, participation and equality — have evolved over a long period of historical time and have been designed to govern Canadian cultural development in the present and the future. While these principles occasionally conflict, they help to anchor Canadian cultural development in reality and give it a strong operational core.

Since artists and arts organizations must be free to follow their instincts wherever they take them, freedom of expression is the most essential principle on which Canada's system of cultural administration is based. This principle manifests itself in a number of ways. First, it manifests itself in an adjudication system where funding decisions are made primarily by professionals and peers on the basis of artistic and cultural criteria rather than by bureaucrats and politicians on the basis of political and economic criteria. Second, it manifests itself in a highly diversified system of financial support — a system which prevents the piper from calling the tune because many sources of support are available. Third, it manifests itself in cultural agencies situated at arm's length from government and the political process. Finally, and most importantly, it manifests itself in the free flow of cultural works across domestic and international borders, rather than through protective measures designed to prevent the free flow of cultural works and shut out cultural products from other parts of the world.

If commitment to freedom is one principle on which Canada's system of cultural administration is based, commitment to excellence and creativity are others. There is little room in Canada for mediocre standards, regardless of whether this involves the creation, distribution or consumption of cultural works. However, care should be taken not to confuse excellence and creativity with elitism. Whereas elitism confines cultural works to a small and select segment of the population, excellence and creativity make it possible for every Canadian to enjoy works of the highest standard of creation and performance.

Whereas commitment to freedom, excellence and creativity are principles that derive largely from the cultural community, commitment to access, participation and equality are principles that derive largely from the political community. Both are essential in a well-designed cultural system. For although it is an established fact that governments have no right to interfere with cultural processes and products, they have every right to ensure that tax-payers dollars are used efficiently and Canadians can participate fully in cultural life. In order to do this, they must ensure that no Canadian is deprived of access to cultural products or processes as a result of age, gender, educational, economic, social and geographical barriers. Not only is it governments' right to expect this, but also it is their responsibility to demand it as a dispenser of public funds.

KEY CULTURAL PROBLEMS

Although Canada possesses a large and dynamic cultural sector, an effective system of cultural administration and a strong set of principles to govern cultural development, Canadians cannot afford to be complacent about the cultural problems facing the country. Indeed, irreparable harm could be done if these problems are not confronted and solved in the future.

Although some problems tend to come and go with the alternating periods of expansion and consolidation which characterize Canadian cultural development, others are more chronic and systemic in nature. Most prominent among these latter types of problems are: the adverse socio-economic condition of Canadian artists and arts organizations; fundamental deficiencies in Canadian content, particularly in the media; the Americanization of Canadian culture through the inflow of cultural products and processes from the United States; insufficient opportunities for cultural education; confusion over multiculturalism and its role in Canadian development; and last but far from least, the crisis of national unity and identity. These problems have been affected in recent years by numerous economic, political, demographic, social and technological factors, as well as by downsizing, cost-cutting, deficit reduction, globalization, unemployment, political uncertainty and free trade.

No problem is more invidious or persistent than the problem of the adverse socio-economic condition of Canadian artists and arts organizations. Despite the rapid growth of the cultural sector over the last century and particularly over the last fifty years, the country's artists and arts organizations are still required to carry the bulk of the burden of support for Canadian cultural development. This they do in numerous ways. First, they do it through low wages, inadequate working conditions, and serious financial problems. Not only are the country's artists among the lowest paid workers in Canada[5] — next to old-age pensioners near the bottom end of the income scale — but also the conditions under which they work often leave much to be desired. Second, they do it through a great deal of unemployment, underemployment, and seasonal employment. Unlike workers in most other professions, artists can face unemployment, underemployment and seasonal rates several times the average. Finally, they do it through inadequate social security benefits. Whereas workers in other professions receive unemployment insurance and workers' compensation when they are injured or out of work, and are usually able to look forward to reasonable pensions and health care benefits, a significant number of Canadian artists do not enjoy these benefits. This is because they are self-employed rather than institutionally-employed, and as such, are not entitled to receive the social security benefits most Canadians take for granted.

A number of attempts have been made in recent years to rectify this situation. For example, at the federal level, the **Task Force Report on The Status of the Artist** recommended numerous changes aimed at improving the socio-economic condition of artists in Canada.[6] Included among its many recommendations were: establishment of a National Advisory Committee on the Status of the Artist; collective bargaining rights for artists; more effective copyright legislation; workers' compensation; more effective unemployment insurance coverage; and improved tax measures. Most prominent among the tax measures were: recognition of the dual employment status of artists as employees and/or self-employed workers for income tax purposes; establishment of a certain level of non-taxable income; income averaging; and permission for artists to use the modified accrual method for accounting and tax purposes.[7] While some progress has been made since the completion of the **Task Force Report**, such as the creation of a National Advisory Committee on the Status of the Artist, establishment of a Canadian Artists and Producers Professional Relations Tribunal, and most recently, improvements in copyright legislation,[8] the socio-economic condition of Canadian artists and arts organizations has not dramatically changed. In fact, if anything, it has worsened as a result of cuts in government expenditure, downsizing, fallout from the free-trade agreements, globalization, and competition from other forms of entertainment. Clearly improvements in the socio-economic condition of the country's artists and arts organizations are mandatory if Canadian cultural development is to thrive in the future. Without a strong cultural community able to enjoy the same socio-economic status and benefits as other Canadians, it is difficult to see how Canada will experience a healthy, productive and vigorous cultural life in the future.

Ensuring a strong cultural community and a healthy, productive and vigorous cultural life are imperative if deficiencies in Canadian content are to be overcome.

Some impressive gains have been recorded in this area in recent decades. For example, many more plays by Canadian playwrights are now available for presentation on the country's theatrical stages compared to three or four decades ago. Moreover, many more books by Canadian authors are available in the country's book stores — up from 31,000 titles in 1991 to 42,000 titles in 1997.[9] Despite this, it is still not common to hear compositions by Canadian composers in the country's concert halls, although it is more commonplace to see paintings by Canadian painters in the country's galleries.

It is really in the cultural industries that deficiencies in Canadian content show up most clearly. Here, the picture is a very disturbing one, as illustrated by the following quotation:

> Ninety-six per cent of the movies that appear in our cinemas are foreign, most of them American. Four out of five magazines sold at our newsstands are foreign, most of them American. Three- quarters of the television we watch every night is foreign, most of it American.
>
> Seventy per cent of the content on Canadian radio stations is non-Canadian, most of it American.[10]

This pattern of heavy foreign and especially American content is even bleaker when attention is shifted to ownership and control of the cultural industries in Canada.[11] Not only does the lion's share of the revenue which accrues to the cultural industries flow out of Canada to finance cultural development elsewhere, largely in the United States, but also, apart from broadcasting, Americans own or control the bulk of the cultural industries in Canada. The reason for this is clear. Americans own or control most of the movie theatres and publishing and recording companies in Canada.[12] When this fact is considered in conjunction with the statistics presented earlier, it is clear why there is so much concern about "the Americanization of Canadian culture." This concern has been fuelled in recent years by the increased flow of American cultural products into

Canada following the signing of the North American Free Trade Agreement, as well as by concerted attempts on the part of American producers to eliminate the cultural exemption from the Agreement.

These problems are compounding at the same time that major shortcomings are showing up in cultural education in Canada. Due to cuts in public expenditure and government grants, many educational institutions are being forced to reduce their commitment to arts and cultural courses and programmes. This is true not only at the university and community college level, but also at the elementary and secondary school level. These reductions are occurring at a time when there is a growing need for more courses and programmes in the arts and culture, as well as for much more cross-cultural education, communication and exchange. Without major initiatives to increase cultural understanding among Canada's diverse ethnic communities and regions, Canada will not be in the strongest position to confront the challenges and opportunities of a society that is increasingly multicultural and multiracial in character.

These initiatives are imperative in view of the confusion that exists throughout the country over multiculturalism and its role in Canadian development. As the century and the millennium draw to a close, it is clear that attitudes toward the country's present policy of multiculturalism are very mixed. On the one hand, there are those who believe that the policy of multiculturalism is one of the country's greatest assets. They contend that it opens up unlimited opportunities for Canadians to learn more about the cultures of others, as well as for different ethnic groups to maintain their cultural roots, traditions and identities. On the other hand, there are those who believe the policy of multiculturalism is one of the country's greatest liabilities. They contend that it creates barriers and divisions between Canadians, acts as a tool for assimilation, marginalizes the concerns of groups such as the native peoples, and prevents Canada from developing a strong sense of national unity and identity. Clearly the current confusion and ambivalence over multiculturalism will have to be addressed in the future if

Canada is to thrive in the years and decades ahead. Not only do common sense and necessity demand it, but logic and justice compel it.

Like the confusion which exists over multiculturalism, there is also a great deal of confusion over national unity and identity.[13] Views and opinions are mixed on both sides of the unity and identity issue.

As far as national identity is concerned, there are those who believe it is best achieved by taking the "melting pot approach." They contend the emphasis should be on identifying and asserting a set of values and beliefs which all Canadians share in common, regardless of ethnic origins, socio-economic status, educational level, or geographical location. They point to the United States as a country which has built up a strong sense of national identity by employing the melting pot approach. In contrast, there are those who believe the melting pot approach would be anathema to Canada and Canadians. They contend that national identity is best achieved through the "mosaic approach." Here, the emphasis should be on preserving differences rather than promoting similarities — encouraging groups, peoples and regions to maintain their distinct values, traditions, beliefs and characteristics rather than surrounding them to a homogeneous culture. The link between identity and multiculturalism is most conspicuous here. It is intimately tied to questions of subsidies and grants for multicultural activities on the one hand and preservation and assertion of a set of common values and customs on the other hand.

Like national identity, views and opinions are mixed on both side of the national unity equation. On the one hand, there are those who maintain that national unity is best achieved by preserving the Constitution in its present form, since this assures a real measure of equality for all provinces, regions and people and prevents any province, region or people from achieving too much "special power." On the other hand, there are those who maintain that national unity is best achieved by creating a new Constitution, one which recognizes Quebec as an unique society and

Quebecers as a distinct people and guarantees the preservation of Quebec's language, culture and identity. It is in this domain that the connection between politics and culture shows up most clearly. Not only is this issue highly charged at present, but also it perpetually threatens to tear the country apart. Clearly ways will have to be found to deal with this exceedingly complex and difficult issue in the future if the country is to remain intact.

PERCEPTIONS OF CANADIAN CULTURE

It is impossible to complete this portrait of the present situation without examining the way in which the country's governments perceive and define Canadian culture. For how Canadian governments perceive and define Canadian culture has a crucial bearing on everything else. For example, perceiving and defining Canadian culture in terms of the arts, heritage and cultural industries has very different implications for Canadian development, relations between Quebec and the rest of Canada, the division of federal-provincial powers, the free trade agreement, the allocation of public funds for cultural purposes and the preservation of cultural values, identities, traditions and beliefs than perceiving and defining Canadian culture in terms of a total way of life or all aspects of life and living in Canada.

Throughout the period from Confederation to the Centennial, Canadian governments solved this most endemic problem of all by perceiving and defining Canadian culture largely in terms of "the arts and heritage." As indicated earlier, the "cultural industries" were added to the list later, largely in recognition of the impact these industries are having on cultures, countries, communication and people everywhere in the world at present. For purposes of these definitions, the arts are usually defined to include music, theatre, dance, mime, painting, sculpture and literature; heritage is usually defined to include art galleries and museums; and the cultural industries are usually defined to include publishing, radio, television, film, video, and sound recording. There has always been a great deal of debate over whether "popular" as well as "classical" activity should be included in these definitions, as well as whether libraries, archives, the crafts, multiculturalism, architecture, town planning, sports, recreation and citizenship should be included in, or excluded from, these definitions. However, this is usually what is meant by Canadian culture when the term is used in political, governmental and corporate circles,[14] reported on in the media, talked about at national and international conferences, written about in official publications, dealt with for purposes of free trade agreements, and promoted abroad.[15] This practice has become even more prevalent with the signing of the North American Free Trade Agreement. Protecting Canadian culture for purposes of the Agreement means protecting the arts, heritage and the cultural industries.

While these perceptions and definitions of Canadian culture have served to bring the country to its present point, there is no doubt that there is a much broader array of perceptions and definitions of Canadian culture in use throughout Canada today. While governments, the media and trade negotiators perceive and define Canadian culture as the arts, heritage and the cultural industries, many scholars, educational institutions, professional associations and special interest groups perceive and define Canadian culture in other ways. These ways run the whole gamut of possibilities, from multiculturalism, recreational activity and shared values, traditions and beliefs to a state of mind, a way of life, and a means of interacting with the natural environment.[16] This makes it essential to come to grips with the many different perceptions and definitions of Canadian culture which are employed throughout the country today.

Changes taking place at the international level, and particularly at UNESCO, may prove helpful in this regard. As indicated earlier, after several decades of perceiving and defining culture in terms of the arts, heritage and cultural industries, UNESCO has started to perceive and define culture in significantly broader terms, especially following the Second

World Conference on Cultural Policies in Mexico City in 1982. The justification for adopting a significantly broader definition of culture was set out in the planning documents and working papers for the World Decade for Cultural Development (1988-1997):

> Without neglecting the importance of creativity as expressed in intellectual and artistic activity, they (participants at the Mexico City Conference) considered it important to broaden the notion of culture to include behaviour patterns, the individual's view of him/herself, of society, and of the outside world. In this perspective, the cultural life of a society may be seen to express itself through its way of living and being, through its perceptions and self-perceptions, its behaviour patterns, values systems and beliefs.[17]

No sooner was the much more expansive view of culture endorsed than it started to have an impact on the Canadian situation. Not only was Canada a signatory to the significantly broader definition of culture adopted by the member states of UNESCO in Mexico City in 1982, but also the following statement was made by Flora MacDonald in 1987 when she was Minister of Communications, Canada's federal department of culture at the time:

> "Culture" is a concept with many different meanings. It certainly refers to artistic and literary activity. But it also has sociological and anthropological connotations — bringing to mind the ways in which societies and groups communicate and, indeed, define themselves.
>
> Canadian culture encompasses all these things. Ultimately, it is the substance and reflection of who we are and what we form as a people. Our landscape is part of it; our tastes, our languages, our pastimes, the way we view the world, these all enter in.[18]

Are there grounds for casting Canadian culture in such expansive terms? Surely there are. When Canadians talk about being "the products of their culture" today, they tend to mean they are the products of everything that exists in their society. This includes not only the arts, heritage and cultural industries, but also economic systems, political processes and ideologies, recreational and educational endeavours, social customs, religious beliefs, spiritual convictions and interactions with the natural environment.

Adoption of this much more all-inclusive way of looking at Canadian culture could prove timely as the country prepares to confront one of the most difficult and demanding periods in its history.

In the first place, it would make it possible for Canadians to see their culture as a "whole," rather than as a series of disconnected and fragmented parts. This could have important implications for the problems Canada and Canadians are confronted with at present, as it would provide a way of looking at and dealing with these problems which transcends social, linguistic, regional, demographic, political and geographical differences and brings Canadians together rather than splits them apart.

Second, it would facilitate the inclusion of many activities that are presently excluded from Canadian culture when the term is used in a political or governmental sense — activities which many Canadians may deem to constitute the very essence of their culture. Most conspicuous among these activities are sports like hockey, figure-skating, curling, rowing, basketball and lacrosse, recreational pursuits like canoeing, skiing, ice fishing and snow-mobiling, social programmes like health care and day care, transportation and communication endeavours like railroads and long-distant satellites, economic practices like mining and the extraction industries, and environmental preferences like love of nature and landscape. To contend that Canadian culture can be perceived and defined without reference to these and other fundamental aspects of Canadian life is not only misleading, but also it represents a serious distortion of reality.

Third, it would promote an understanding of Canadian culture which is consistent with the country's historical development, contemporary situation and future needs. Without this, it is difficult to see how Canada and Canadians will escape becoming more and more enmeshed in the cultural definitions, perceptions, practices and policies of other countries, particularly countries like United States which have a strong understanding of their culture and the reasons for promoting, cultivating, exporting and asserting it.

Finally, it would make it possible to confront many of Canada's most deep-seated cultural problems head on in government and the political process. This is because Canadian culture would be given a status, stature and priority it has never received in the political process. The reason for this is apparent. Canadian culture would be treated as a mainstream rather than marginal activity and made the centrepiece and principal preoccupation of Canadian development. Such a commitment may be necessary if problems as severe as national unity and identity, maintenance of Canadian cultural sovereignty, improvement of the welfare and well-being of all Canadians, overcoming the adverse socio-economic condition of Canadian artists and arts organizations and achieving unity in diversity are to be addressed successfully in the future.

THE CHALLENGE OF THE FUTURE

> If in Canada, with all our resources of wealth and talent, we cannot work together to share our heritage of wisdom and values, our views of reality and ways of expressing them, it will be because we have missed what may well be the central meaning of our federation. For surely a confederation exists to make it possible for us to create our own life and environment... It could be the potential stimulus of a living and vital culture that connects us with each other and all of us with our memories of the past and our dreams of the future.[1]
>
> Bernard Ostry

If the complex connection between culture and politics is to be dealt with effectively in the future, it will be necessary to come to grips with a number of issues inexorably linked to the country's political and cultural life. Foremost among these issues are: the need for a holistic understanding of Canadian culture; establishment of the requisite historical base; construction of an east-west cultural axis; creation of an effective global cultural system; and realization of a new political awareness with respect to the role of Canadian culture in Canada's future development and the lives of all Canadians. Time spent analyzing these issues is rewarding because it helps to open the doors on a broader and deeper way of looking at culture and politics in Canada and the complex connection between them.

A HOLISTIC UNDERSTANDING OF CANADIAN CULTURE

The time is ripe for a holistic understanding of Canadian culture. Not only would it help to expand awareness of the vital importance of Canadian culture at a crucial time in the country's development, but also it would enable Canadians to come to grips with the nature and meaning of their culture and the reasons for cultivating, promoting, protecting and developing it.

The key to a holistic understanding of Canadian culture lies in the realization that Canadians have come together in historical and geographical association for the purpose of living together in the world and working out their association with the world. In the process, they have created a culture which has been compelled to confront a whole series of difficult challenges. How is the world seen and interpreted? How is survival guaranteed? How is the need for food, clothing, shelter, health, welfare, jobs, income, spiritual renewal and aesthetic expression dealt with? How are environmental, economic, political, social, educational and religious systems developed? How are communities, regions, and the country as a whole organized? How is physical space occupied? How is the quality of life improved? And how are relations conducted with other countries, other peoples, other cultures, the natural environment, and the world at large? In other words, how is a culture created which meets the needs of Canadians for survival, security, fulfillment and well-being?

While culture in the holistic sense constitutes the core of Canadian development, it is much more implicit than explicit at present. Nevertheless, there is much to be gained by making it explicit at this time, especially as it focuses attention on those factors and forces which are most instrumental in shaping Canadian development and fulfilling the needs of Canadians.

When Canadian culture is visualized in holistic terms, it is concerned with the entire way Canadians perceive and interpret the world and act in the world. Taking a cue from this, Canadian culture can be defined as "a dynamic and organic whole" which is concerned with the way Canadians "visualize and interpret the world, organize themselves, conduct their affairs, elevate and embellish life, and position themselves in the world."[2]

Every part of this holistic definition sheds a great deal of light on the nature, meaning, character and substance of Canadian culture.

How Canadians visualize and interpret the world deals with all those cosmological, philosophical, mythological, theological, scientific, aesthetic, ethical and ideological beliefs which Canadians possess. These beliefs constitute the cornerstone of Canadian culture because how Canadians visualize and interpret the world determines in large part how they develop their culture in the world. As such, they deserve the highest priority and utmost attention because they relate so fundamentally to what Canada and Canadians are all about.

How Canadians organize themselves deals with all the decisions Canadians make with respect to economic systems, political processes, social structures, technological practices, communications' networks, electronic and information highways, and the development of towns, cities, regions, and the country at large. Whether the country is organized as a "community of communities," a "nation of nations" or a "federation of provinces, regions and territories" — as well as whether the country is organized along liberal, conservative, socialist or capitalist lines — are all matters which fall within the purview of how Canadians organize themselves in space and time.

How Canadians conduct their affairs deals with the character of Canadians' lives, and with it, decisions about consumer practices, consumption expenditures, investments, family life, education, child rearing, living arrangements, and the like. A great deal of information exists on this particular facet of the country's culture as a result of census data, statistical collections, opinion polls, consumer surveys, and studies undertaken by specialized agencies and professional associations.

How Canadians elevate and embellish life deals with all the decisions Canadians make with respect to artistic, social and spiritual practices, religious beliefs and ideals, recreational and leisure-time activities, intellectual pursuits, and moral and human concerns. Many of these decisions are instrumental in making life a fuller, richer, healthier, and more meaningful affair than it would otherwise be.

And how Canadians position themselves in the world deals with all the decisions Canadians make with respect to relations with other countries, cultures and people, as well as Canada's diplomatic posture, geographical position, and territorial manoeuvring in the world. Included here are activities related to the negotiation and signing of trade agreements, foreign affairs, developmental assistance, peace-keeping, and diplomatic arrangements. When Northrop Frye said the most important question facing Canadians is not "who are we?" but "where is here?," he was focusing on the crucial importance of "place" in Canada's overall geographical and geopolitical positioning in the world.

When Canadian culture is perceived and defined in these terms, it can be visualized as a huge tree with roots, branches, leaves, flowers and fruit.[3] Metaphorically speaking, myths, legends, theology, philosophy, history, ethics, cosmology and aesthetics constitute the roots; economic systems, technological practices, political ideologies, social structures, environmental policies and consumer practices constitute the trunk and branches; and artistic activities, religious and scientific beliefs, educational systems, recreational activities, literary works and spiritual ideals constitute the leaves, flowers and fruit.

The implications of this metaphorical depiction of Canadian culture are clear. If Canadian culture is to be developed effectively in the future, it must be developed at every level. While this is essential at the level of the trunk and branches — that is to say at the economic, commercial, financial, technological and political level — it is equally essential at the level of the roots, leaves, flowers and fruit — that is to say at the cosmological, philosophical, scientific, artistic, educational, ethical and spiritual level. For just as every component part of the tree plays an indispensable role in the overall functioning of the tree as a dynamic and organic whole, so every component part of Canadian culture plays an indispensable role in the overall functioning of the country's culture as a dynamic and organic whole.

When it is visualized and defined in this way, all individuals and institutions are part of Canadian culture. It is as much the concern of the farmer in Saskatchewan, the fisherman in Newfoundland and the logger in British Columbia as it is the artist in Ontario, the business woman in Quebec, the teacher in New Brunswick, and the banker in Nunavut. Moreover, it cuts across every sector of society, from business, industry, commerce, trade and technology to government, recreation, education, health, welfare, the arts, religion, and the environment. Not only does every individual, institution and sector of society have a fundamental stake in Canadian culture when it is viewed in this way, but also every individual, institution and sector of society has a valuable contribution to make to it.

What is true for individuals, institutions and sectors of society is equally true for groups, regions, peoples, and cultures. All groups, regions, peoples and cultures in Canada — be they of aboriginal, French, English, German, Ukrainian, Scandinavian, Jewish, Indian, Italian, Chinese, Brazilian, Jamaican, Japanese or Sudanese origin or any other origin — have a valuable contribution to make to Canadian culture as well as a fundamental stake in it. Not only is Canadian culture receiving countless contributions every day from all the individuals, institutions, sectors of society, groups, regions, peoples and cultures which comprise it, but also it is receiving numerous contributions from every town, village, city, urban centre, province and region in the country. It is this fact that makes Canadian culture a mosaic rather than a melting pot — a diverse and multi-textured whole which is greater than the sum of its parts by virtue of the fact that new qualities and properties have been created in the whole which are not in the parts.

Canadian culture is concerned with two matters of fundamental importance to Canada and Canadians when it is visualized in this way. The first is **worldviews,** or the ways Canadians visualize and interpret the world and position themselves in the world. The second is **values,** or the specific weights and priorities that Canadians assign to the component parts of the country's culture.

Putting the emphasis on worldviews and values cuts to the bone of Canadian culture because it focuses attention on how Canadian culture is positioned in the natural, historical and global environment, as well as how the component parts of the country's culture are ordered, orchestrated and put together to form a whole. Without much more analysis and discussion of these matters, Canada and Canadians could easily experience higher levels of environmental pollution, ecological degeneration, social, political and labour unrest, demands for sovereignty association, and a declining rather than rising standard of living. It is an unpleasant prospect, but one which is predictable if the appropriate actions are not taken to prevent it.

THE REQUISITE HISTORICAL BASE

Of all the actions which are required to deal with Canadian culture in holistic terms, none is more essential than the need to establish a proper historical foundation on which to predicate future developments. Without an effective historical base, it is difficult to see how Canadian culture will be able to make its full contribution to the realization of a better Canada and a better world.

The key to establishing this base lies in interpreting Canadian history from a cultural rather than economic, technological or political perspective. The reason for this is clear. While Canadians have had many economic, technological and political needs to attend to over the centuries, they have likewise had many other needs to attend to as well. It is the multifarious nature of these needs — social, artistic, educational, spiritual, recreational, scientific and environmental as well as economic, technological and political — which gives rise to a cultural interpretation of Canadian history and the realization that Canadians have come together in historical and geographical association for the purpose of building a culture.

Viewed from this perspective, four "historical facts" stand out without a shadow of a doubt. First, the origins and roots of Canadian culture are aboriginal, not European. Second, the native peoples of Canada are the "founding peoples" of Canadian culture. Third, all of Canada's diverse peoples and ethnic groups have made substantial contributions to Canadian cultural development. And fourth, Canadian culture has a long and distinguished tradition. Examination of these facts helps pave the way for establishment of a strong historical base on which to predicate future developments.

Recognition of the fact that the origins and roots of Canadian culture are aboriginal rather than European is imperative if Canada's historical base is to be set properly. For despite the fact that Europe and Europeans played a crucial role at a particular stage in the country's development, the origins and roots of Canadian culture are aboriginal not European. This has important implications for Canadian development in the future because it focuses attention on the need to recognize the seminal contributions of the Indian and Inuit peoples of Canada to the genesis of Canadian development, with all this implies for everything that comes thereafter.

For thousands of years prior to the arrival of the Europeans, the Indians and Inuit were busy attending to numerous needs and requirements. And they did so in precisely the same manner as the Europeans did centuries later, namely by fanning out across the great "Dominion of the North" and scattering pockets of settlement wherever the environment proved compatible. In the process, they developed technologies in such fields as exploration, transportation, communication, habitation and navigation which were indispensable for penetration into the interior of the country by the Europeans. Without the kayak, umiak, canoe, dog sled, snowshoe, long house and teepee, the history of Canada — and indeed the entire history of North America — would be very different from what it is today. In addition to this, the Indians and Inuit developed agricultural, artistic and craft activities, modes of social organization and security, systems of government, and political practices like democracy which have had an important bearing on Canadian culture and Canadian politics — as well as the cultures and politics of other countries — over the last four centuries.[4] Finally, and perhaps most importantly, the Indians and Inuit evolved worldviews, values, and forms of spirituality and social bonding which reveal a profound understanding of the intimate connection between human beings, nature and other species, the need for environmental protection and preservation, and the importance of living in harmony with the natural environment and each other. These worldviews, values, and forms of spirituality and social and ecological bonding need careful study today because they may hold the key to future directions in Canadian development.

It is for reasons such as these that Canadians are anxious to see an improvement in the lives and circumstances of the native peoples. This was confirmed most recently during the **Citizens' Forum on Canada's Future,** where an overwhelming majority of participants in the **Forum** expressed an interest in seeing a resolution to aboriginal land claims and self-government for the native peoples.[5] It is attitudes like these, particularly when they are combined with aggressive lobbying by the Indians and Inuit themselves and practical proposals like those contained in the Berger and Dussault-Erasmus Commissions,[6] which point the way to the future. For they signal the need to recognize the seminal contributions the native peoples have made — and continue to make — to Canadian culture in the country's political enactments, educational endeavours and historical narratives.

If the native peoples made indispensable contributions to the opening up of Canada and indeed the entire North American continent, so did the French. Not only did the French make numerous contributions to penetration into the interior of the country and the continent through explorations by explorers like Cartier, Champlain, Radisson, La Vérendrye, Jolliet and others, but also they established their position at the cutting edge of Canadian culture at Port Royal, Quebec and Montreal. It is a position they have maintained right up to the present day as documented earlier. There is ample evidence of this in the agricultural, industrial, artistic, social and educational accomplishments emanating from Quebec and French Canadians in other parts of Canada. While these achievements need to be much better known and utilized in all parts of the country, who is not exceedingly grateful to the French for the rich contributions they have made to Canadian culture in both an historical and contemporary sense? It is for reasons such as these that protection of French language, culture, law and tradition is imperative in the future.

What is true for the French is also true for the English, Scotch, Irish and Welsh. Like the contributions of the French, contributions by immigrants from England, Scotland, Ireland and Wales — and their descendants — span the whole gamut of possibilities, from government, trade, politics, medicine and commerce to music, literature, drama, science, education and the arts. And what is true for people from England, Scotland, Ireland and Wales and their descendants is equally true for people from the Ukraine, Italy, Finland, Poland, Germany, Iceland, Sweden, Greece, Portugal and elsewhere in Europe and their descendants. It is this fact that gives Canadian culture a European and Judeo-Christian cast in both a historical and contemporary sense:

> Despite a long history of the migration of peoples from every corner of the globe and the unmistakable contributions and impact of this rich "melange" to the unique character of Canadian culture, yet the building blocks of our culture are firmly planted in the world view of Western European civilisation. Many of the crowning achievements of our Canadian culture emerge from the interface of the British and French presence with this vast and awesome Canada.

> Our institutional infrastructure, the way our country works, and our power base, is still largely of British

origin in particular, French in Quebec. Judeo-Christian ethics, mores and beliefs still underlie our institutions and community life.[7]

... A walk through any Canadian town or city reveals the unique juxtaposition of church, courthouse, townhall, school, banks and shops and residential streets characteristic of a European ordering of priorities.[8]

If it is essential to recognize the historical and contemporary contributions made by Canadians of European origin and background, it is equally essential to recognize the historical and contemporary contributions made by Canadians of Asian, African, Latin American, Caribbean and Middle Eastern origin and background. These contributions have steadily increased as more people from these parts of the world have flowed into Canada in recent years.

Although Canada's policy of multiculturalism is recent, multiculturalism is deeply rooted in Canada's cultural and political life. The facts of the matter reveal that many groups and peoples from other parts of the world than Europe made significant contributions to Canadian cultural development between 1650 and 1997, and particularly between 1800 and 1997. For example, the Chinese played a crucial role in the building of the Canadian Pacific Railway, Sikhs and East Indians made seminal contributions to the opening up of the British Columbian timberlands, especially in the latter part of the 19th century, and Canada became an important terminus for the Underground Railway in the late nineteenth century. "Towns like Buxton became model black communities producing the first black lawyers, school teachers and preachers in North America. The first Black civil war commander came from Buxton. The first female editor of a newspaper in North America, Mary Shadd Cary was a Black woman who made her way to Canada during this period."[9] It is facts like these that have made Canada a world leader in multiculturalism and social and equity legislation. Not only did Canada abolish slavery before Great

Britain and the United States, but also the country's Bill of Rights and Charter of Rights and Freedoms are contemporary manifestations of the historical battle Canadians have waged to deal with ethnic, linguistic and cultural differences in an equitable manner.[10] It is historical accomplishments and precedents like these which have helped to open the doors to Canada's current policy of multiculturalism within a bilingual framework, as well as to immigrants from Africa, Asia, the Middle East, South America, and the Caribbean. Descendants of these immigrants, along with new arrivals, have made an indelible mark on Canadian culture.

It is the fact that Canadian culture has received substantial contributions in an historical and contemporary sense from immigrants from all parts of the world and their descendants, as well as from the native peoples, which gives Canadian culture its diverse and dynamic character. While only a small sampling of these contributions is possible here, they are epitomized in the works of painters like Légaré, Paul-Émile Borduas, Emily Carr, Helen Lucas, Guido Molinari, Kazuo Nakamura, Norval Morrisseau, Tom Thomson and Ashoona Pitseolak, writers like Oliver Goldsmith, Susanna Moodie, Pauline Johnson, Frederick Phillip Grove, W. O. Mitchell, Gabrielle Roy, Stephen Leacock, Robertson Davies, Rohinton Mistry, Neil Bissoondath, Joy Kogawa, Michael Ondaatje and Nino Ricci, composers like Calixa Lavallée, Healey Willan, Alexina Louie, Harry Freedman, Violet Archer and John Weinzweig, playwrights like Lescarbot, Michel Tremblay, Tomson Highway and Sharon Pollack, architects like Douglas Cardinal, Eberhard Zeidler, Arthur Erickson and Moshe Safdie, singers like Gilles Vigneault, Salome Bey, Gordon Lightfoot, Sarah McLachlan, Teresa Stratas, Ben Heppner and Buffy Sainte-Marie, musicians like Guy Lombardo, Oscar Peterson, Louis Lortie and André Laplante, film-makers and photographers like Norman McLaren, Claude Jutra, Denys Arcand, Frederic Back, Atom Egoyan, Roloff Beny and Yousuf Karsh, athletes like Tom Longboat, Jean Beliveau, Gordie Howe, Donovan Bailey, Myriam Bédard, Carolyn Waldo, Jacques Villeneuve and Silken Laumann, inventors like Abraham Gesner, Alexander Graham Bell, Frederick Banting, Charles

Best and Lap-Chee Tsui, scholars like Harold Innis, Northrop Frye and Marshall McLuhan, politicians like John A. Macdonald, Wilfrid Laurier, Casimir Gzowski, Lester Pearson, David Lewis, Pierre Elliott Trudeau, Lincoln Alexander and Roy Romanow, humanists and social activists like Nellie McClung, Norman Bethune, Jean Vanier, Terry Fox and Ric Hansen, environmentalists like Archibald Stansfield Belaney, Jack Miner, Ernest Thompson Seton and John Macoun, broadcasters like Peter Gzowski, Pamela Wallin and Barbara Frum, and businessmen and entrepreneurs like Samuel Cunard, Armand Bombardier, H. Harrison McCain, Kenneth Colin Irving, Ed Mirvish and Garth Drabinsky.

If it is important to set the record straight on the contributions made by people of every ethnic background and racial origin to the historical and contemporary development of Canadian culture, it is also important to set the record straight on how these contributions get woven into the fabric of Canadian culture and make important statements about the country's cultural life, even if they may draw on worldviews, values, roots and identities established elsewhere.

To illustrate this point, take the artistic and literary works of an artist like William Kurelek. While there is no doubt that Kurelek's paintings draw heavily on his Ukrainian background and heritage, his paintings nevertheless speak to Canadians about their own cultural reality, especially the cultural reality of the Prairies. And what is true for Kurelek's paintings is equally true for his literary works. Books like **A Prairie Boy's Winter**, **A Prairie Boy's Summer**, **Lumberjack** and **A Northern Nativity** are integral parts of Canadian culture because they speak to Canadians about a reality with which they can readily identify. And what is true for an artist like William Kurelek and his works is equally true for a scientist like David Suzuki and an architect like Raymond Moriyama and their works. Both these talented individuals draw on the Japanese heritage and its well-known sensitivity for ecology, nature and landscape. However, programmes like **The Nature of Things** and architectural edifices like the Ontario Science Centre are

Canadian icons because they speak to Canadians about their own ecological relationship with "the land" or the natural environment. Is there not something about the way the Ontario Science Centre tumbles down the side of a hill and **The Nature of Things** takes Canadians into the far reaches of Canadian geography that cuts to the bone of Canadian culture?

While immigrants and their descendants often draw on worldviews, values, traditions and beliefs shaped in other parts of the world, these worldviews, values, traditions and beliefs enrich, strengthen and challenge Canadian culture because they infuse Canadian culture with new ways of looking at, interpreting, and understanding Canada's own reality. The process starts soon after immigrants arrive in Canada and commence their lives in a new and often difficult social, economic, political, educational and geographical environment. While the process of cultural adaptation and change is often very painful and may take a long period of time to evolve due to a variety of factors — social, linguistic, demographic, economic and political — immigrants and their descendants adjust to the new reality by making contributions which over time take on more and more of the characteristics of the new environment in which they find themselves, even if they draw on worldviews, values, traditions and beliefs created elsewhere. Bhikhu Parekh makes this point in talking about the intimate connection between immigrants, ethnic groups, multiculturalism, the creation of public spaces, and the new cultural reality immigrants and ethnic groups find themselves in:

> Multiculturalism doesn't simply mean numerical plurality of different cultures, but rather a community which is creating, guaranteeing, encouraging spaces within which different communities are able to grow at their own pace. At the same time it means creating a public space in which these communities are able to interact and enrich the existing culture and create a new consensual culture in which they recognize reflections of their own identity.[11]

This point has a great deal of relevance for the way Canadian culture has developed in the past and should be developed in the future. For while much more research needs to be undertaken on this fundamental feature of Canadian cultural life, it is not a case of developing Canadian culture **or** specific cultures in Canada. Rather it is a case of developing both, but developing them in such a way that Canadian culture provides the context within which specific cultures are situated. Since this is a non-coercive process in Canada since Canada does not possess an official culture or expect immigrants and ethnic groups to assimilate into a homogeneous melting pot, "integration" rather than "assimilation" is always the key. This makes it necessary to focus attention on the way specific cultures in Canada — be they of French, English, Italian, Polish, African, Asian or Caribbean origin or any other origin — are positioned in and enrich Canadian culture as a dynamic and organic whole. Presumably this is what it means to say that "every ethnic group has the right to preserve and develop its own culture and values **within the Canadian context**."[12]

While Canada does not have an official or homogeneous culture, it does have a number of "commonalties of experience" and "values" which Canadians tend to share as a group. These commonalties of experience and values — which help to give shape, substance, character and direction to the country's cultural life — have been created by Canadians of countless different backgrounds, origins and experiences over the centuries. They include, in addition to others: dedication to a land of great beauty, size and grandeur; commitment to freedom and equity regardless of race, gender, age, colour, creed or disability; devotion to social security and health care; recognition of the rights, traditions and beliefs of others; belief in democracy, equality and fairness; commitment to consultation, dialogue, accommodation and tolerance; support for regional and ethnic diversity; compassion and generosity; and commitment to freedom, peace and non-violence.[13] Commonalties of experience and values such as these were confirmed most recently in the **Citizens' Forum on Canada's Future** which brought together Canadians from all parts of the country, walks of life, and

84

ethnic backgrounds.[14] According to the Commissioners of the **Forum**, these values and commonalties of experience should provide the well-spring for Canadian identity in the future.

It is impossible to consider commonalties of experience and values as essential as these without considering another key component in Canadian cultural history. It has to do with the pivotal role heritage plays in Canadian development and national unity and identity.

Recognition of this fact is imperative if the historical base is to be set properly for Canada's future development. This is what makes the work of institutions like the Historic Sites and Monuments Board, the Royal Society of Canada, the Canadian Historical Association, Parks Canada, the Canadian Museum of Civilization, the CRB Bronfman Foundation, the Heritage Tourism Secretariat, the Canadian Tourism Commission, the Department of Canadian Heritage — and their provincial and municipal affiliates and counterparts across the country — so essential. Institutions like these, and numerous others, are performing an exceedingly valuable function by making Canadians more aware of the country's historic sites, parks and conservation areas, heritage river systems, century-old buildings, railway stations, festivals, fairs, and cultural attractions. The Department of Canadian Heritage, the Heritage Tourism Secretariat and the Canadian Tourism Commission have been particularly active in this area in recent years promoting greater interest in Canadian heritage and tourism in general and cultural heritage and tourism in particular.[15] Their efforts are being rewarded in both a cultural and economic sense, as Canadians learn more about their historical roots and traditions and expenditure on Canadian tourism increases rapidly.

These activities help to make Canadians more aware of the fact that the country's culture has a long and distinguished tradition. It is a tradition that stretches back to the earliest days of Indian and Inuit settlement and concludes with the multicultural and multiracial reality so conspicuous today. This helps to bring to an end some erroneous views that have gained currency in the country in recent years. One is that Canada was a "cultural wasteland" prior to the arrival of the Europeans. Another is that Canadian culture is a post World War II phenomenon. Neither view has any foundation in historical fact. For the facts of the matter reveal that Canada has a vital and vibrant past — a past which needs to be much better known and utilized by all Canadians. While Canada may be a comparatively new country in a political sense, it is anything but a new country in a cultural sense. In a cultural sense, it possesses roots, origins, traditions and achievements stretching back thousands of years.

CONSTRUCTION OF AN EAST-WEST CULTURAL AXIS

With the proper historical base in place, it is possible to proceed to the next priority in Canadian development. It has to do with the construction of an east-west cultural axis capable of linking the country and its citizenry together and making it possible for all Canadians to enjoy, experience, participate in and share their culture.

If Canadian culture is to thrive in the future, an east-west **cultural** axis is mandatory. Not only is creation of such an axis the key to overcoming the divisions which exist between the various regions, provinces, ethnic groups and peoples of the country, but also it is the key to helping Canadians know and understand themselves, each other, the world around them, and the threads which bind them together as a society. Not coincidentally, it is also the key to coming to grips with the country's most demanding and debilitating problems, particularly the need for social cohesion, national unity and identity, too much reliance on American culture and programming; and the adverse socio-economic condition of Canadian artists and arts and media organizations.

Here too, history has much to teach which is relevant to the future. For history teaches that Canadians have confronted — and overcome —

their most complex and debilitating challenges by creating east-west axes against virtually insurmountable odds. In the sixteenth, seventeenth and eighteenth centuries, there was the creation of an east-west explorations' axis. It was created to provide the basis for European penetration into the interior of the country. In the nineteenth century, there was the creation of an east-west transportation axis. It was created to facilitate the flow of raw materials and manufactured goods from the Atlantic to the Pacific. Canals like the Rideau and railroads like the Canadian National and Canadian Pacific played the crucial role here. In the twentieth century, and particularly in the latter part of it, there has been the creation of an east-west communications' axis. It has been constructed to facilitate the movement of people, products, resources, information, messages and ideas over long distances in short periods of time. In this case, planes, trucks, telephones, radio, television and cable systems, newspapers, films, electronic highways, satellites, internets and the like have played the prominent role, as companies like Air Canada, Bell Canada, the Canadian Broadcasting Corporation, the National Film Board, the Globe and Mail, the Canadian Press Service, Baton Broadcasting, Rogers Cable and others confirm. These east-west axes have been required to overcome the natural contours of North American geography, which, as every Canadian knows only too well, are north-south rather than east-west.

What is needed in the twenty-first century — and needed more than ever — is an east-west **cultural** axis. Such an axis must prove capable of moving Canadian materials of all kinds — books, films, plays, paintings, musical compositions, radio and television programmes, videos, resources, commodities, groups, ideas, publications, natural resources and manufactured goods — across the country in volumes heretofore unknown in Canadian history. In the construction of this axis, maximum consideration should be given to materials which deal with the country's own cultural reality.

The country's artists, scientists, architects, educators, theatre and dance companies, symphony orchestras, art galleries, museums, libraries, publishing and film houses, radio and television stations, research institutes, educational institutions and the like have a pivotal role to play in the realization of this axis. These are the individuals and institutions which possess the communications' skills and sensorial and intuitive abilities which are necessary to convey vital information about Canadian culture as a dynamic and organic whole which cannot be communicated at all in another way, or cannot be communicated nearly as effectively using another device. This they are able to do through their ability to create the signs, symbols, stories, myths, metaphors, legends, rituals and research which "stand for the whole" through a dramatization or over-representation of the parts of the whole.[16]

While national institutions like the Canadian Broadcasting Corporation, the National Film Board, the Canadian Museum of Civilization, the National Gallery of Art, the National Museum of Science and Technology, the National Museum of Natural History and others have an extremely important role to play in the creation of this axis,[17] many other institutions have a key role to play as well. As indicated earlier, many of the country's smaller theatre and dance companies, artist-run centres, musical organizations, film houses, small presses, video co-operatives, educational and scientific organizations and the like have created repertoire that deals specifically with Canadian content and Canada's own cultural reality. While the content and reality of other countries is important because it brings fulfillment to millions of Canadians each year and helps to broaden and deepen understanding of the strengths and shortcomings of Canadian culture, it is Canadian content and Canada's own cultural reality that needs to be much better known and appreciated in Canada. This is the content and reality which deals with the country's own domestic and international challenges and opportunities, as well as creates the links which are necessary to bind Canadians together in space and time. Far too often, "world premieres" of Canadian works are not followed up by measures to ensure that these works become permanent fixtures on the cultural scene. As a result, the country and its citizenry are not being served to best advantage by the rich legacy of artistic, heritage, media, scientific and educational resources successive generations of Canadians have struggled to create.

While the country's artists, educators, architects, film-makers, arts, media and heritage organizations, educational institutions and the like have a seminal role to play in the construction of an east-west cultural axis, they are not the only individuals and institutions required to perform this role. Numerous business people, health care providers, researchers, doctors, lawyers, farmers, volunteers, labourers, corporations, foundations, professional associations and the like also have a crucial role to play in the construction of this axis. Not only are they important contributors to Canadian culture as a dynamic and diverse whole, but also they possess the skills and abilities which are necessary to make Canadian cultural resources and accomplishments much better known, appreciated and utilized in Canada. While these skills and abilities may be much in demand in other parts of the world due to globalization and the emergence of a "borderless world," sight should never be lost of the fact that these individuals and institutions possess many of the capabilities and talents which are needed to strengthen cultural development at home.

In thinking about the kind of cultural axis most needed for the future, sight should not be lost of the vital contributions that Quebec, Quebecers, the native peoples, and multicultural and multiracial groups are able to make to the development of this axis.

As indicated earlier, Quebec, Quebecers and French Canadians generally occupy a prominent position at the cutting edge of Canadian culture due to their high regard for culture and its role in public and private life. Over the centuries, they have created a vast reservoir of experience and expertise in cultural creation, policy, development and administration which needs to be much better know and utilized in Canada. While language acts as a barrier to utilization of a certain part of this reservoir, now that many more Canadians are bilingual, much more effective use could and should be made of the reservoir of acumen that Quebec artists, arts administrators, researchers, civil servants, and departments and institutes like the Ministère de la Culture et des Communications du Québec, l'Institut québécois de recherche sur la culture and l'Institut national de la recherche scientifique possess in abundance. Not only would this help to confirm the value which Quebec, Quebecers and French Canadians attribute to culture, but also it would help to confirm the crucial role culture plays in the formation of individual and group identity.

While the initiative for taking advantage of this rich cornucopia of capabilities should come from "the rest of Canada," it should be reciprocated by Quebec, Quebecers and French Canadians. If a true "dialogue of cultures" is to be achieved in Canada, initiatives on the part of Canadians of non-French origin and background must be matched by their French counterparts and particularly by Quebec and Quebecers. The way French and non-French hockey players have collaborated in bringing home countless international honours for Canada should serve as a source of inspiration in this regard. Numerous achievements on all cultural fronts are possible if this potential for collaboration and excellence is harnessed and utilized fully.

What is true for Quebec, Quebecers and French Canadians is equally true for the native peoples, multicultural and multiracial groups and associations, and indeed all provinces, regions and cultures in the country. Every people, group, association, province, region and culture in Canada possesses a vast reservoir of acumen and expertise to contribute to the construction of an east-west cultural axis. While a significance part of this contribution involves preserving and protecting roots, traditions, identities and distinctive features, a significant part of it also involves sharing these precious treasures with other Canadians. And what better way to do this than to participate in the construction of an east-west cultural axis which draws on the insights, experiences and expertise of all provinces, regions, cultures, groups and peoples in the country. Not only would this help to broaden and deepen cultural values and commonalties of experience and reduce the risk of cultural conflict, but also it will help to integrate all provinces, regions, cultures, groups and peoples more fully into Canadian culture.

It is difficult to see how a cultural axis can be constructed on the scale envisaged here without maximum involvement on the part of the public sector and the private sector, as well as effective collaboration between them.

All governments in Canada have a key role to play in this. First, they can provide the leadership that is necessary to ensure that creation of an east-west cultural axis is given the highest priority in public policy and decision-making. Second, they can provide the funding that is necessary to ensure that Canadian products, publications, ideas, artefacts and groups are able to criss-cross the country in volumes large enough to be meaningful. Many of the institutional mechanisms, structures and precedents needed for this are already in place. For example, the federal government has already negotiated a number of "cultural development agreements" with certain provinces; most provincial governments now operate exchange programmes with other provinces in specific sectors of cultural life; and many municipal governments have twinning arrangements with other municipal governments across the country. What is needed now, and needed on a much more massive scale, is the financial commitment to building on these institutional mechanisms, structures and precedents. Such a commitment would help to ensure that Canadians in all parts of the country are able to profit from Canadian creations in all fields of cultural endeavour. Third, governments can ensure that exchange programmes and agreements are based on **reciprocal** movements of people, products, ideas and artefacts. This is necessary to ensure that all parties gain through mutual association and enrichment. Finally, and perhaps most importantly, governments can see to it that as many barriers to cross-country circulation and exchange as possible are reduced or eliminated. This applies not only to reduction or elimination of trade and other kinds of commercial encumbrances, but to reduction or elimination of social, environmental, scientific, artistic and educational barriers as well.

If governments have a strong role to play in the construction of an east-west cultural axis, so do corporations, foundations and financial institutions. Banks, insurance companies, manufacturing ventures and community and family foundations should be equally involved in providing the leadership, funding, exchange programmes and initiatives which are necessary to link the country and its citizenry together in a cultural sense. While many of these institutions have been involved in funding organizations, institutions, agencies and programmes in their own localities, few have been involved in providing funding to move cultural works to other parts of the country. A major campaign to realize this could work miracles in terms of ensuring that Canadian cultural creativity in all its diverse forms and manifestations is accessible to all Canadians on a sustained and systematic basis.

While governments, corporations, foundations, financial institutions and professional associations have a pivotal role to play in this process, the most important role is reserved for Canadians. Canadian cultural creativity will not flow through the arteries of Canada to the extent it should until Canadians make a full-scale commitment to it. It is the same kind of commitment which Canadians have demonstrated time and again when they have been confronted with major difficulties or natural disasters, as recent responses to the eastern Canadian ice storm and the Saguenay and Red River crises confirm. It is amazing how Canadians can come together during difficult times to help their fellow citizens in other parts of the country. It is this kind of commitment which is now needed to build an east-west cultural axis equal to the challenge.

CREATION OF A GLOBAL CULTURAL SYSTEM

In much the same way that the most essential challenge in a domestic sense facing Canada and Canadians is to build an east-west cultural axis capable of linking the country and the citizenry together, so the most essential challenge in an international sense is creating a global cultural system capable of projecting Canadian culture abroad and receiving cultural projections from abroad.

There must be no mistaking what this means in fact. On the one hand, it means projecting Canadian culture to other parts of the world in all its diverse aspects and manifestations — artistic, educational, scientific, social, economic, commercial, financial, political and technological. This constitutes the **"out-going"** dimension of Canada's global cultural system. On the other hand, it means receiving cultural projections from other parts of the world in all their diverse aspects and manifestations. This constitutes the **"in-coming"** dimension of Canada's global cultural system. It is only when these two dimensions are fully developed and in balance that it is possible to claim that the country has created a global cultural system equal to the task.

Given the importance of achieving this state of affairs in the country's international cultural life, it is essential to determine how people in other parts of the world form their understanding of Canadian culture as a whole. Surely they form it in exactly the same way Canadians form it, namely through exposure to parts of the whole which "stand for the whole" and are "symbolic of the whole." Thus, in much the same way that artists, educators, humanists, athletes, arts, media and athletic organizations, educational institutions and the like play an indispensable role in helping Canadians to get to know and understand their culture as a dynamic and organic whole, so they play an indispensable role in helping others to get to know and understand this whole. It is through exposure to the aesthetic accomplishments of the Indians and the Inuit, the artistry of the Group of

93

Seven, Mary Pratt, Alex Colville, Jean-Paul Riopelle and Bill Reid, the writings of Pierre Berton, Farley Mowat, Margaret Atwood, Antonine Maillet and Lucy Maud Montgomery, the music of Harry Somers, the Nova Scotia Symphony, L'Orchestre symphonique de Montréal and the Winnipeg Symphony, the songs of Alanis Morisette, Céline Dion, Bryan Adams and Anne Murray, the presentations of the Canadian Opera Company and Le Cirque du Soleil, the scientific accomplishments of Bertram Brockhouse and John Polanyi, the skating of Kurt Browning, Catriona LeMay Doan and Elvis Stojko, the heroics of Roberta Bondar, Marnie McBean and Wayne Gretzky, the grit and determination of countless Canadian hockey, curling and rowing teams, the efforts of organizations like the International Development Research Centre, the Organization Canadienne pour la Solidarité et le Développement, AFS Interculture Canada, the Canadian Executive Service Organization and Canada World Youth/Jeunesse Canada Monde, television programmes like **Ann of Green Gables** and **The Road to Avonlea,** and manufacturing goods like those produced by Bombardier Inc., Northern Telecom Limited and McCain Foods Ltd. — to cite only a handful of the individuals, institutions and works which represent Canadian culture abroad — that an understanding of Canadian culture starts to take shape in the minds and imaginations of people and countries in other parts of the world. And what is true for people and countries in other parts of the world is equally true for Canadians. Canadians form their understanding of other cultures through exposure to parts of the whole which stand for the whole and communicate vital information about the whole. It follows from this that the cultures of other countries will really only be known and appreciated in Canada, and Canadian culture will only be known and appreciated abroad, when there is much more emphasis on the role artists, athletes, scientists, educators, humanists and their institutions and works play in helping Canadians to understand other cultures and people in other countries to understand Canadian culture.

If the only reason for placing artists, athletes, scientists, humanists, educators and their institutions and works in a position of pivotal importance in the development of Canada's global cultural system was because they perform the holistic function required to know and understand cultures as dynamic and organic wholes, they might be dismissed more readily as forces to be reckoned with in the future. However, there are other compelling reasons as well. They have to do with the fact that it is the works of these talented individuals and institutions which enhance Canadian identity abroad, reduce fears that come from an inability to understand the signs and symbols of others, and deal with "the human factor" in development. Without doubt, Canada should be interacting first and foremost in those areas which give the most human and humane expression to the country's most creative cultural accomplishments. These are the activities which expose the real face of Canadian culture to people and countries in other parts of the world, thereby opening the doors to a much more human, humane, harmonious and people-centred approach to international development.

They also open the doors to numerous trade, commercial, industrial, financial, technological and diplomatic possibilities:

> Canada's arts and cultural industries play a central role in projecting our image as an open, dynamic and creative nation. This can only enhance our performance in the larger political and economic arenas. A cultural image sells itself, its country and its products. Culture opens the doors to international trade.[18]

While much is made of the "Team Canada" missions of the federal government and their ability to produce billions of dollars in contracts for Canadian companies, little attention is paid to the prerequisites which are necessary for this. Many of these prerequisites have been created by the country's artists, humanists, educators, scientists and athletes through previous projections of Canadian culture abroad. Take trade and economic relations with China as an example. It is highly unlikely that Canadian companies would be able to profit from business opportunities in China had it not been for humanists like Norman Bethune who worked for years helping the Chinese through a very difficult stage in their development, artists like Maureen Forrester who gave so generously of her time and talent to conduct numerous workshops for Chinese singers and musicians, and comedians like Mark Rowswell who is rapidly becoming a legend as Dashan or "Big Mountain" in China.[19] And what is true for Canada's relations with China is equally true for Canada's relations with other countries. The Canadian economy, Canadian companies and Canadians generally profit from numerous economic, business, financial, technological and trade opportunities with other countries because people and countries in other parts of the world have already formed an impression of Canadian culture through the works of Canadian artists, scientists, architects, scholars, athletes, educators and their institutions. As John Ralston Saul so forcefully argues:

> Canada's profile abroad is, for the most part, its culture. That is our image. That is what Canada becomes in people's imaginations around the world. When the time comes for non-Canadians to buy, to negotiate, to travel, Canada's chance or the attitude towards Canada will already have been determined to a surprising extent by the projection of our culture abroad.[20]

Given this fact, much more attention should be focused on the way Canadian culture is projected abroad in the future. On the one hand, this means determining how the country's culture can be projected more effectively to other parts of the world. On the other hand, it means determining how countries and people in other parts of the world profit most from projection of Canadian culture abroad.[21]

Canadian culture can be projected more effectively to other parts of the world by expanding the country's network of contacts with other countries, strengthening the marketing, managerial and financial capabilities of Canadian creators, producers and distributors, and evolving a system of international relations which is just, equitable and humane.

Expanding Canada's network of contacts with other countries will not be possible without a quantum leap in the country's international relations. Whereas the focus of Canadian development has largely been internal up to the present point, primarily to harness the natural resources of the country and make it fit for habitation, increasingly the focus should be international as well as domestic. The reason for this is not difficult to detect. Not only is Canada entering "a global era" in its development, much like many countries in the world, but also the welfare and well-being of Canadians will depend primarily on the ability of Canadians to function effectively in the international domain in the future. This has important policy implications for the country's governments at all levels, but particularly for the federal government. Without strong leadership from the federal government, Canada will not be able to increase its network of contacts with other countries of the world, project its culture abroad effectively, and maintain its privileged position in the world. Not only must Canada continue to maintain strong links with traditional allies like France, Great Britain, the United States and the Commonwealth, but also it must develop strong relationships with African, Asian, Latin American, Middle Eastern and Caribbean countries as well as La Francophonie.

Strengthening the marketing, managerial and financial capabilities of Canadian creators, producers and distributors in all fields of cultural endeavour should go a long way towards realizing this. A page from the country's artistic history may prove helpful here. When Canada's performing arts organizations were experiencing difficulty developing their audiences in the late nineteen sixties and early nineteen seventies, an international authority was brought in to assist them with their subscription sales and audience development.[22] Most performing arts organizations are still reaping the benefits of this. Not only have they substantially increased their subscription sales and audience base, but also their financial stability and fiscal situation is much improved. It is expertise like this which is now needed to strengthen the projection of Canadian culture across the board, as well as to sell Canadian cultural products in other parts in the world. Although history has demonstrated that Canadians can compete with the best the world has to offer when they are not put at a disadvantage due to the economies of large-scale production and insufficient markets and financial resources, Canada's creators, producers and distributors in the arts, education, the media, technology, and business need assistance in strengthening their global marketing, administrative and financial capabilities if they are to compete on the world scene. By providing the best expertise available, the country's governments could supply the support that is needed to enable Canada to make its full mark on the world.

Development of a system of international relations which is just, equitable and humane is indispensable for this. It requires the ability to play an impartial and independent role in the world, as well as to assert values and qualities which are deeply ingrained in Canadian culture. This will not be easy in view of the fact that Canada's system of international relations is deeply embedded in a global system which is strongly influenced by financial and commercial interests and powerful countries. Viewed from this perspective, it is not sufficient to engage in international relations for the purpose of improving Canada's material standard of living, overcoming domestic resource deficiencies, expanding consumer choice, buying and selling products, capitalizing on numerous economic, political, technological and trade opportunities, and developing artistic, educational, athletic and spiritual abilities. It is also necessary to engage in international relations for the purpose of making the world a better and safer place for all. This means strengthening efforts to maintain peace, order and stability in the world, as well as helping the less fortunate peoples and countries of the world.

Canada is ideally equipped to execute this role. In the first place, the country possesses a great deal of credibility in the world as a result of its willingness to confront difficult social, multicultural, linguistic, economic and geographical problems. While these problems have not always been dealt with successfully, and while Canada has its own share of social, political, ethnic and racial shortcomings, the very fact that Canadians have had the determination to try and address these difficulties places Canada and Canadians in an ideal position to contribute to global development and international understanding. Secondly, Canadians have engendered a great deal of trust and respect in the world as a result of their willingness to engage in peace-keeping endeavours and measures to improve stability, order and security in the world. Thirdly, Canada possesses a great deal of creativity and expertise in those very areas which are of greatest demand in the world, especially transportation and communications' systems, resource development, health care, education, telecommunications, social affairs, technology and the arts. Finally, Canadians possess many of the characteristics which are most needed in the world today, including perseverance, tolerance, generosity, civility, respect for the needs and rights of others, and ability to make concessions and compromises. While care must be taken not to over-represent these capabilities or pretend that Canadians do not possess their share of shortcomings and limitations, there is no doubt that these characteristics place Canada in a strong position to make a crucial contribution to the realization of a more equitable, just and humane world.

It is for reasons such as these that Canadians should pay careful attention to how people and countries in other parts of the world benefit when Canadian culture is projected abroad. Surely they benefit most when Canada's global cultural system is based on caring and sharing, concern for people, and human welfare and well-being. In order to achieve this, it is necessary, among countless other things, to: increase foreign aid and developmental assistance as a percentage of gross national product; develop the policies and practices which are needed to redistribute surplus food, clothing, building materials, supplies and staples to countries in the less fortunate parts of the world; share natural resources more liberally and broadly; reduce international debt loads, particularly among Asian, African and Latin American countries; and contribute to improved social, medical and health capabilities throughout the world.

Of all the contributions Canada can make to people and countries in other parts of the world, none may be greater than drawing on the assets and abilities that other countries possess in abundance. Utilization of these assets and abilities is not only the key to overcoming the imbalances and inequities which currently exist throughout the world, it is also the key to developing relations which mutually enrich all countries.

Canada will have to substantially improve its capacity for receiving cultural projections from abroad if it is to achieve this. A number of developments at home in recent years suggest that things are moving in a positive direction in this regard. First of all, Canada is in a much stronger position to receive cultural projections from abroad as a result of its multicultural and multiracial population, particularly parts of the world like Africa, Asia, Latin America, the Caribbean, the Middle East and La Francophonie with which Canada has had little contact in an historical sense. Secondly, many more foreign business and political delegations, educational groups, research associations, artists and arts organizations are visiting Canada each year. Mention should be made here of domestic and international activities like the International Festival of Authors, World of Music, Arts and Dance (WOMAD), Festival International de la musique Orford, Celebrating African Identity (CELAFI), Vancouver International Folk Festival, Calgary International Jazz Festival, Newfoundland Sound Symposium, Winnipeg New Music Festival, Caravan, Caribana, Desh Pardesh, the Banff Television Festival and others which help expose Canadians to international artistic achievements. Finally, and perhaps most importantly, many countries are establishing cultural centres and foreign studies programmes in Canada. These centres and programmes are especially important because they provide a wide range of activities and expose Canadians to other cultures on a more sustained and systematic basis. It is developments like these that augur well for the future. For they help to balance the in-coming and out-going dimensions of Canada's international relations while simultaneously recognizing that people and countries in other parts of the world play an indispensable role in the development of Canada's global cultural system.

A NEW POLITICAL AWARENESS

A new political awareness is necessary if culture is to make a significant contribution to the realization of a better Canada and a better world.

There is much to be learned from present political perceptions and ideologies which is relevant to the realization of this awareness. For present political perceptions and ideologies are based largely on the conviction that culture plays a marginal rather than mainstream role in Canadian development. Evidence of this fact is not difficult to provide. In domestic terms, culture is usually viewed as a component part of the Canadian economy. When the economy is in a state of buoyancy, government funding for culture may be increased, but often at a nominal or modest rate. When the economy is in a state of recession or is undergoing difficulty, government funding on culture is almost invariably cut back. This is particularly true when conservative political ideologies prevail, much as they do at present. In this case, culture is viewed primarily as a private sector activity expected to make its way in the marketplace.

What is true in a domestic sense is also true in an international sense. Stripped to its essence, Canada's current system of international relations is based on the conviction that Canada engages in international relations largely for the purpose of advancing its economic, commercial, financial, technological, trade and political interests. Since relations are more difficult to conduct between countries than within countries — primarily because of differences in worldviews, values, traditions and beliefs — ways have to be found to overcome these difficulties. "International cultural relations" provide the perfect vehicle in this regard. Perceived and defined largely in terms of the arts, academic affairs, athletic activities, and more recently the "cultural industries" of publishing, radio, television, film, video and sound recording — that is to say the way most governments in Canada and the Department of Foreign Affairs and International Trade view international cultural relations — international cultural relations are seen as the supplements that are needed to advance Canada's economic, commercial, financial, technological, trade and political interests. While this view is starting to change,[23] it is a view that is still firmly entrenched in the minds of most politicians, bureaucrats, governments and foreign policy experts.

The origins of this ideology can be traced back to the seventeenth and eighteenth centuries and the age of mercantilism, the geographical explorations, and the rise of nation states. By the middle of the nineteenth century, conditions were ripe for this ideology to move from the wings to centre stage on the world scene. Not only was economics becoming the centrepiece of national and international development, but also economies were becoming the principal preoccupation of governments and politicians.[24] Moreover, the economic interpretation of history was rapidly gaining ground and winning converts. It was a rendering of the process of historical evolution based on the conviction that economics and economies should be given precedence over everything else because they are the "cause" of everything else.[25]

While economics and economies have dominated national and international thinking over the last two centuries, a number of developments throughout the world indicates that preoccupation with economics and economies may be inadvisable in the future. The costs, consequences and dangers may be too great.

First of all, preoccupation with economics and economies leads to material demands and expectations which are impossible to fulfill in view of the size and growth of the world's population and the carrying capacity of the earth. Secondly, consumption practices are condoned which have a devastating effect on the natural environment and people's lives, largely by increasing pollution and environmental breakdown and making it difficult for people to deal with "the crisis of maldevelopment" or spiritual poverty in the midst of plenty. Thirdly, the gap between rich and poor countries and rich and poor people is increased, thereby enhancing the potential for a great deal more unrest, conflict and confrontation. Fourthly, "the human factor" is extremely difficult to deal with because the focus is on economics and material interests and concerns. Finally, and most importantly, people build cultures when they come together in historical and geographical association as illustrated earlier in the case of Canadian culture. While economies are a very important part of this because they are concerned with people's material needs and consumption requirements, they are only one part of a much larger process. People have a variety of needs which must be attended to if they are to function effectively in society. These needs give rise to a complex set of social, spiritual, aesthetic, recreational, medical, educational, political, technological and economic requirements.

It follows from this that economies are component parts of cultures rather than the reverse. The implications of this are clear. Culture and cultures, rather than economics and economies, should be made the principal preoccupation and centrepiece of domestic and international development. Not only is it necessary to develop strong economies and effective commercial, financial, fiscal and technological capabilities, but also it is necessary to develop strong social, educational and health programmes, environmental and political policies, artistic and scientific practices, and recreational and spiritual activities. Presumably this is why the Dutch cultural historian, Johan Huizinga, contended that "the realities of economic life, of power, of technology, of everything conducive to man's material well-being, must be balanced by strongly developed spiritual, intellectual, moral and aesthetic values."[26] Surely this is the most effective way to ensure that concern for people, the natural environment, future generations, and especially caring and sharing become the principal preoccupations of politics and decision-making.

It is now clear why there is such an intimate connection between culture and politics. Both are concerned with "the whole," and therefore with ensuring that the parts of the whole are properly situated and balanced in the whole. In order to achieve this for Canada, it is necessary to give Canadian culture a status and stature in political affairs and government policies that it has not received in the past. Indeed, the country's culture should be made the centrepiece of Canadian politics and development and dealt with accordingly. The implications of this are clear. Governments and politicians will have to abandon their penchant for thinking about Canadian culture in marginal and specialized terms and start thinking about Canadian culture as the very essence and raison d'être of their existence; parliaments and cabinets will have to devote much more time to discussing the development of Canadian culture in all its diverse aspects and manifestations; departments of cultural development will have to become the key departments in government; cultural models will have to become the main vehicles of political and governmental decision-making; and cultural policy will have to be accorded the highest priority in public policy.

Viewed from the comprehensive perspective provided by Canadian culture, it is not a case of developing Canadian culture **or** developing the Canadian economy. Rather it is a case of developing both, but developing them in such a way that the Canadian economy is properly positioned in Canadian culture. Despite the vast importance of the Canadian economy to the country and its citizenry, what must be constantly borne in mind is the fact that the Canadian economy is a part of the whole and not the whole itself. Without proper positioning in the whole, the Canadian economy will serve commercial, financial, technological and material interests rather than human and environmental interests.

Positioning the economy properly in Canadian culture would help to ensure that the Canadian economy is pointed in the right direction in the future. Rather than functioning as an autonomous entity in its own right, the economy would be constrained and enriched by the broader cultural container in which it is situated. This would help to ensure that the more specific goals of economics and the Canadian economy — consumption, investment, productivity, growth, profits, competition and the marketplace — are constrained and enriched by the broader and deeper goals of culture and Canadian culture: excellence, creativity, caring, sharing, respect for the rights of others, the natural environment and future generations, and especially commitment to people and the human factor in development.

Pressing cultural rather than economic goals to the forefront of public policy could prove valuable and timely. On the one hand, it could help to reduce the drain and strain on scarce renewable and non-renewable resources and the natural environment because more emphasis would be placed on the qualitative side of development and hence on activities like the arts, education, learning, social interaction, spiritual renewal, conservation and permanence which make fewer demands on the resources of nature. On the other hand, it would help to enhance the Canadian economy by placing more emphasis on co-operation, job, income and resource sharing, training, creativity, excellence and diversity than on competition, consumption, exploitation, and survival of the fittest. This is imperative in an age characterized by environmental degeneration, globalization, transnational capital movements, free trade, oppressive debts, and high levels of unemployment and under-employment, especially among the country's young people.

Just as the Canadian economy needs to be properly positioned in Canadian culture if it is to function effectively, so all the component parts of Canadian culture should be properly positioned in this way. For example, technology and communications should be properly positioned in Canadian culture if they are to serve human and environmental interests rather than commercial and financial interests. And what is true for technology and communications is equally true for health and welfare, education, the arts, religion, science and social activities. All component parts of Canadian culture should be properly positioned in the whole if they are to serve Canada and Canadians to best advantage in the future.

This need for balance and positioning must be matched by some very specific initiatives on the part of the country's federal, provincial and municipal governments. While a great deal of debate, discussion, research and analysis needs to take place on this, four key areas must be addressed if Canadian culture is to be developed effectively in the future. These four areas are: the development of effective models, tools and techniques to solve particular types of Canadian cultural problems; protection of Canadian culture from **undue** foreign competition and influence, especially from the United States; a great deal more education in Canadian culture; and last but far from least, recognition of the central role of culture in Canadian development and the lives of all Canadians. Time spent examining these four areas helps to provide the avenues and insights which are necessary to organize and orchestrate the complex connection between culture and politics in the future.

If Canada is to be successful in building a dynamic and vital culture in the future, much more attention will have to be focused on the development of effective models, tools and techniques to solve particular types of Canadian cultural problems.[27]

While the country's governments have recourse to a broad range of models, tools and techniques to deal with problems in Canadian culture — economic models, social models, grants, subsidies, regulation, legislation, taxation, programmes, information, statistics and the like — most of these models, tools and techniques place more emphasis on the "supply side" than the "demand side." As indicated earlier, the country's governments have demonstrated a marked preference for economic models, grants and subsidies to solve problems in key sectors of Canadian cultural life, such as the arts, heritage, and the cultural industries. While this is consistent with the belief that "supply creates its own demand" and the practices of many European countries, it is doubtful if it will serve Canada and Canadians to best advantage in the future, particularly now that broader meanings of culture and Canadian culture are making their appearance on the scene.

What is needed here more than anything else is the development of a comprehensive **cultural model** capable of capitalizing on the best features of the supply and demand approaches. While there is a need to increase the supply of Canadian cultural works through grants and subsidies — especially in the arts, heritage, the cultural industries, education and health care which are unable to make ends meet in the marketplace and are of such vital importance to Canadian unity, identity and sovereignty — the real challenge is on the demand side. While this ultimately depends on changed attitudes and practices on the part of Canadian consumers and citizens, the country's governments could play a valuable role here by stimulating much more demand for Canadian works of all kinds. Included among the many measures needed to achieve this are: more purchases and commissions of Canadian works and products; improved tax treatment for creators, producers and consumers; elimination of as many barriers to cultural participation and sharing as possible; a variety of ticket and product stimulation schemes; improved marketing and distribution techniques; and many more opportunities for cross-country fertilization and exchange.

These measures would help to ensure that Canadian culture and Canada's creators, producers and consumers are protected from **undue** foreign influence and competition, especially from the United States. For a dramatic increase in the demand for Canadian cultural materials and the size of the market for Canadian cultural products would make it possible to counteract the increased flow of American cultural works into Canada. Where this is not possible, governments should act forcefully to protect

Canadian culture from too much foreign competition, control and ownership, especially in key sectors like publishing, television, film, video, sound recording, the performing and exhibiting arts and health care which speak to Canadians about their own cultural reality and are of vital importance to the country's future development. While Canada's long-term interests are best served by developing the marketing, managerial and financial capabilities of Canadian creators, producers and distributors to the point where they can compete with their counterparts from other parts of the world, the country's short-term interests are best served by ensuring that Canada's creative talents are not placed at a disadvantage due to the economies of large-scale production and more favourable financial conditions elsewhere. Despite pressure from American producers and organizations like the Organization for Economic Cooperation and Development, key sectors of Canadian cultural life should be protected in all future trade agreements until Canada has developed its domestic and international marketing, managerial and financial capabilities to the point where a healthy balance is achieved between Canadian and non-Canadian activity. This is especially imperative in any future free trade agreements, as well as in agreements like the Multilateral Agreement on Investment which threaten to undermine the country's ability to speak to itself about its own way of life.

It is impossible to discuss the country's capacity to speak to itself about its own way of life without raising the related issue of education. Since culture lies at the root of many of the country's most difficult and demanding problems — tensions between different regions and provinces, relations between Quebec and the rest of Canada, the crisis of national unity and identity, the aspirations of the native peoples, the Americanization of Canadian culture, interactions with the natural environment and the preservation of Canadian values and ideals — it is impossible to ignore the educational requirements of culture. Without much greater attention to Canadian culture in the country's school system, the country and its citizenry could face significant hardships in the future.

Although Canadian culture is not an easy subject to teach in the country's elementary and secondary schools, community colleges and universities,[28] there are a number of reasons why every Canadian should receive a solid grounding in Canadian culture in the school system. First, Canadian culture lies at the root of national unity and identity. Without a strong understanding of the country's culture, Canadians will lack the bonds and links necessary to keep the country and the citizenry together. Second, Canadian culture is the basis of social cohesion and citizenship, as well as the means whereby immigrants and newcomers are integrated into Canadian society. Third, Canadian culture helps to counteract Americanization and the steady inflow of American cultural products into Canada. Fourth, Canadian culture provides an ideal context within which other disciplines and fields of study can be situated. Finally, Canadian culture holds the key to new environmental realities, worldviews, values and practices, largely by focusing attention on the qualitative as well as the quantitative sides of development.

Broadening and deepening understanding of the role of culture in general and Canadian culture in particular in the country's school system could prove helpful in addressing one of the most difficult political requirements of all. It concerns political recognition of the central role culture should play in Canadian development and the lives of all Canadians.

Clearly the country's governments will have to come to grips with this requirement if Canadian culture is to flourish in the years and decades ahead. Without a strong and dynamic culture and effective sharing of the component parts and diverse cultures which make up this culture, it is difficult to see how national unity, identity and sovereignty will be achieved and maintained in the future. If the country's governments are to be successful in coming to grips with this, it will be necessary to sort out the respective roles and responsibilities of the various levels of government for culture and deal with culture fully in all future constitutional debates and negotiations.

Since culture was not mentioned at all in the BNA Act, there has always been a great deal of confusion and controversy over which level or levels of government should be responsible for it. In a strict, constitutional sense, the federal government is responsible for culture because all areas not specifically designated in the Act are deemed to be the responsibility of the federal government. This helps to explain why the federal government was so involved in the cultural life of the country immediately following Confederation, as well as why Canada possesses a "top-down" rather than "bottom-up" approach to cultural development. In practice, however, all levels of government are and have been involved in the cultural development of the country, and have assumed responsibility for it.

According to many cultural experts, responsibility for culture should be vested primarily — if not exclusively — in the hands of municipal and provincial governments. The reason for this is clear. Culture is first and foremost a "grass roots affair." Northrop Frye frequently made this point in talking about the difference between economic and political development on the one hand and cultural development on the other hand. Whereas economic and political development are highly centralized in nature and national and international in scope according to Frye, cultural development is decentralized in nature and local and regional in character.[29] While Frye was employing the artistic and heritage definition of culture and not the holistic one, his convictions on the decentralized nature of culture are shared by many cultural authorities. Augustin Girard, the renowned French authority on culture, for example, contends that "the decentralization of activities...is at once the first step in the direction of cultural democracy and, at the same time, essential to cultural creativity, vitality and freedom. Thus decentralization is necessarily the guiding principle of cultural democracy."[30] This helps to explains why a country like Germany — which shares many political similarities with Canada as a federal state — prefers to vest responsibility for culture primarily in the hands of the Länder or provincial governments. It also explains why giving more power to the provinces and especially Quebec in such areas such as training and immigration in recent years has helped to diffuse a number of cultural and political tensions in Canada.

In thinking about the way governmental roles and responsibilities for culture should be addressed in the future, no greater mistake could be made than to take a static approach. Since cultural life is changing rapidly in Canada and is being affected by globalization, computerization, commercialization and new international realities, there is a need for a dynamic approach. Such an approach must come to grips with the grass roots and decentralized nature of culture — with all this implies in terms of increased involvement on the part of provincial and municipal governments — as well as with interregional, national and international requirements. It also means coming to grips with the fact that cultural needs exist at every level of governmental activity.

The Task Force on National Unity dealt with this problem by contending that the federal government should look after matters of national cultural importance, provincial governments should look after matters of regional and provincial importance, and municipal governments should look after matters of local and community importance. While this is difficult to achieve in practice because many cultural interests cut across all levels of government, it provides a useful point of departure.

Clearly the federal government will have to play a leadership role if Canada is to be successful in building a culture which meets the needs of all Canadians. Given the rapidly-changing nature of the global situation, it should increasingly be an international, national and interregional role. Not only should the federal government be actively involved in broadening and deepening Canada's cultural contacts with other countries in the world and improving the country's capacity to project its culture abroad and receive cultural projections from abroad, but also it should be actively involved in protecting Canadian culture from **undue** foreign competition, delivering programmes of national significance, and creating an east-west cultural axis capable of improving interregional co-operation, communication and exchange. This will require a quantum leap in funding for sectors like the arts, heritage, the cultural industries, education, health care and science which hold the key to Canadian cultural development in the future.

Provincial governments have an equally important role to play in the cultural development of the country, particularly in terms of preservation and protection of distinct cultures and identities. Just as Canadian culture is a whole, so specific cultures within Canadian culture are "wholes within the whole." These wholes need preservation and protection if they are to survive and flourish in the future, especially in an age when an increasing number of cultures and identities are threatened with diminution, disintegration or extinction due to globalization and the spread of a ubiquitous "global culture." The experience of Quebec, Quebecers and the Quebec government could prove timely here, as they have gone farther than any other province or provincial government in protecting culture and developing the tools and techniques necessary for this.

Municipal government leadership is equally essential if community and local needs are to be addressed properly. This leadership should be focused on the development of towns and cities as cultural resources, identification and nurturing of creative talent, particularly young creative talent, improvements in the capacity of existing institutions to respond to local needs, the development of "cultural districts" and cultural tourism, and generating much more support from corporations, foundations and private benefactors for cultural development. It also necessitates ensuring that municipalities have the fiscal resources and taxation powers which are needed to deal with these requirements successfully.

Sorting out the respective roles and responsibilities of the various levels of government could go a long way towards coming to grips with the constitutional requirements of culture. Clearly culture has evolved in Canada to the point where it must be confronted head-on in all future

112

constitutional arrangements and discussions. What is most needed in this area at the present time is a specific section of the constitution dealing with culture, Canadian culture and Canada's distinct cultures, as well as with the legal, legislative, fiscal and financial requirements which are necessary to protect, preserve and enhance all aspects of Canadian cultural life. Quebec culture and the cultures of the native peoples could then be used as specific examples to illustrate and confirm general principles — general principles which require forceful action and urgent attention because the cultures of the native peoples and Quebec are the most threatened in Canada at the present time. But this is not only a problem for Quebec, Quebec culture, or the cultures of the native peoples. It is a problem for all cultures in Canada, be they in Newfoundland, the Maritimes, British Columbia, the Prairie Provinces, Ontario, the Yukon or the North West Territories.

Constitutional guarantees are imperative if Canadian culture and Canada's diverse cultures are to be preserved, protected and developed in the future. For building a culture based on diversity, sharing, integration and inclusion rather than uniformity, assimilation and exclusion means ensuring that all the various elements which go into making up this culture receive the attention and priority they deserve in all funding allocations, governmental policies, political decisions and constitutional agreements. Ultimately this is what dealing with culture and politics and the complex connection between them is all about.

ENDNOTES

Lead quotation: **Shared Values: The Canadian Identity: Report to the People and Government of Canada.** Ministry of Supply and Services Canada. Ottawa. 1991. pp. 23-24.

CHAPTER I

1. John Meisel. "Political Culture and the Politics of Culture." **Canadian Journal of Political Science.** Vol. 7. No. 4. December 1974. p. 615.

2. The Task Force on Canadian Unity was fully aware of the political and cultural problems involved in achieving and maintaining national unity in Canada. See: The Task Force on Canadian Unity. **A Future Together: Observations and Recommendations.** Ministry of Supply and Services Canada. Ottawa. 1979; and The Task Force on Canadian Unity. **A Time to Speak: The Views of the Public.** Ministry of Supply and Services Canada. Ottawa. 1979.

3. Department of Communications. **Vital Links: Canadian Cultural Industries.** Ministry of Supply and Services Canada. Ottawa. 1987. Also see Paul Audley. **Canada's Cultural Industries: Broadcasting, Publishing, Records and Film.** James Lorimer & Company, Publishers in association with the Canadian Institute for Economic Policy. Toronto. 1983.

4. For a detailed statement of the types of problems encountered in the complex connection between culture and politics and the role of governments in the cultural affairs of nations see: Milton C. Cummings, Jr. and Richard S. Katz (ed.). **The Patron State: Government and the Arts in Europe, North America and Japan.** Oxford University Press. Oxford. 1987. (See in particular the article by John Meisel and Jean Van Loon. "Cultivating the Bushgarden: Cultural Policy in Canada." pp. 276-310).

5. Northrop Frye. **The Bush Garden: Essays on the Canadian Imagination.** Anansi. Toronto. 1971. p. iii.

6. For an examination of the implications of a market, welfare and nationalist approach to Canadian culture see: Thelma McCormack. "Culture and the State." **Canadian Public Policy - Analyse de Politiques.** Vol. X. Number 3. Fall 1984. pp. 267-277.

CHAPTER II

1. Tom Henighan. **The Presumption of Culture: Structure, Strategy, and Survival in the Canadian Cultural Landscape.** Raincoast Books. Vancouver. 1996. p. 140.

2. Maria Tippett. **MAKING CULTURE: English-Canadian Institutions and the Arts before the Massey Commission.** University of Toronto Press. Toronto. 1990. pp. 63-75.

3. **Ibid.** (See Chapter Three on 'A Mad Desire to Bring About State Control': Government Patronage and the Arts. pp. 63-91).

4. Canadian Broadcasting Act. Chapter 24, **Statutes of Canada.** 1936. Ottawa. The King's Printer. 1936.

5. Maria Tippett. **op. cit.** p. 172.

6. Marie Tippett. **op. cit.** p. 173.

7. Canada. **Report of the Royal Commission on National Development in the Arts, Letters and Sciences 1949-1951.** King's Printer. Ottawa. 1951.

8. Bernard Ostry. **The Cultural Connection: An essay on Culture and Government Policy in Canada.** McClelland and Stewart. Toronto. 1978. pp. 79-88.

9. **Ibid.** p. 80.

10. **Ibid.** p. 81-82.

11. **Ibid.** pp. 68-69.

12. Québec. **Livre blanc du Ministère des Affaires culturelles.** Ministère des Affaires culturelles. Québec. 1965. (Laporte Report).

13. Québec. **Rapport de la Commission d'enquête sur l'enseignement des arts.** Éditeur officiel du Québec. Québec. 1966. (Rioux Report).

14. Canada. **Report of the Royal Commission on Government Organization.** Queen's Printer. Ottawa. 1962-1963. (Glassco Report).

15 These revisions represent the first real attempt by the federal government to come to grips with the bureaucratic implications and requirements of culture.

16. It is important to point out that while Canada's policy of multiculturalism is recent, Canada's policy of bilingualism can be traced back to 1849 when all bills of the United Canada Parliament, now Quebec and Ontario, were given assent in both English and French. See: John Robert Colombo (editor). **1997:The Canadian Almanac**. Macmillan Canada. Toronto. 1997. p. 104.

17. Canada. **Report of the Royal Commission on Bilingualism and Biculturalism.** Volumes I-V. Queen's Printer. Ottawa. 1965-1968.

18. Canada. **Report of the Royal Commission on Bilingualism and Biculturalism.** Volume IV. Queen's Printer. Ottawa. 1968.

19. Canada. Parliament. House of Commons. **Debates**. (Hansard). October 8, 1971 as reported in S. M. Lipset. **Continental Divide: The Values and Institutions of the United States and Canada.** Routledge. New York and London. 1990. p. 180.

20. Jean R. Burnet with Howard Palmer. **A History of Canada's Peoples: "Coming Canadians": An Introduction to a History of Canada's Peoples.** McClelland and Stewart in association with the Multiculturalism Program, Department of the Secretary of State and the Canadian Government Publishing Centre, Supply and Services Canada. Ottawa and Toronto. 1988. p 225. (See Chapter Twelve on Multicultural Canada for an excellent history of Canada's multicultural legislation and initiatives between 1968 and 1988).

21. **Ibid.** p. 225.

22. **Ibid.** p. 225.

23. **Ibid.** p. 225.

24. **Canadian Multiculturalism Act**. House of Commons. Ottawa. 1988.

25. D. Paul Schafer and André Fortier. **Review of Federal Policies for the Arts in Canada (1944-1988).** Prepared for the Department of Communications. Canadian Conference of the Arts. Ottawa. 1989. p. 22.

26. **Ibid.** pp. 22-23.

27. **Ibid.** p. 23.

28. UNESCO. **Intergovernmental Conference on Institutional, Administrative and Financial Aspects of Cultural Policies, Venice, 1970.** UNESCO. Paris. 1970.

29. The Department of the Secretary of State was working on a policy for the performing arts when Gérard Pelletier was appointed Minister of Communications in 1972. The policy was never released after Hugh Falconer became Secretary of State in 1972.

30. Canadian Conference of the Arts. **Direction Canada: A Declaration of Canadian Cultural Concern.** Canadian Conference of the Arts. Ottawa. 1973.

31. Québec. **La politique québécoise du développement culturel. Volume I, II and III.** Gouvernement du Québec. Québec. 1978.

32. Bernard Ostry. **op. cit.** p. 160.

33. Québec. **La politique québécoise du développement culturel. Volume I.** op. cit. (A General View: the Culture under Consideration). p. 1.

34. After several decades of defining culture as "the arts, heritage and finer things in life," UNESCO now defines culture in significantly broader terms. See D. Paul Schafer. **The Character of Canadian Culture.** World Culture Project. Scarborough. 1990. pp. 4-50 for a discussion of this, as well as an analysis of the main ways of defining culture in general and Canadian culture in particular.

35. Robert Bailey. **Rapport: The Arts, People and Municipalities.** Canadian Conference of the Arts. Toronto. 1978.

36. See for example: Urwick, Currie and Partners Ltd. **An Assessment of the Impact of Selected Large Performing Companies Upon the Canadian Economy.** Canada Council Information Services. Ottawa. 1974; Department of Tourism. **Stratford Visitors Survey: 1974.** Government of Ontario. Toronto. 1975; S. Book. **Economic Aspects of the Arts in Ontario.** Ontario Arts Council. Toronto. 1974; Nini Baird. **The Arts in Vancouver: A Multi-Million Dollar Industry.** Community Arts Council of Vancouver. Vancouver. 1976.

37. Canada. **Report of the Federal Cultural Policy Review Committee.** Supply and Services Canada. Ottawa. 1982. Also see: Canada. **Federal Cultural Policy Review Committee: Summary of Briefs and Hearings.** Supply and Services Canada. Ottawa. 1982.

38. UNESCO. **Mexico City Declaration on Cultural Policies**. UNESCO. Paris. 1982.

39. D. Paul Schafer. **Canadian Culture: Key to Canada's Future Development.** World Culture Project. Markham. 1995. pp. 1-11.

40. See D. Paul Schafer and André Fortier. **op. cit.** pp. 56-62.

41. The Task Force on National Unity. **op. cit.** 1979.

CHAPTER III

1. Jack Gray. "The Performing Arts and Government Policy" in Anton Wagner (ed.). **Contemporary Canadian Theatre: New World Visions.** Simon & Pierre. Toronto. 1985. p. 31.

2. See for example: Cultural Labour Force Project. **Cultural Sector Labour Force 1991 Census Consortium.** Statistics Canada 1994. p. i; and Culture, Tourism and the Centre for Education Statistics. **The Health and Vitality of the Cultural Sector: Appendix II: Profile of the Arts and Culture Sector in Canada: November 1997.** Statistics Canada. Ottawa. 1997. p. 196.

3. See for example: Canadian Conference for the Arts. **Performing Arts Statistics 1993/94.** Canadian Conference of the Arts. Ottawa. 1995. pp. 1-2. (The statistics are based on data provided by Statistics Canada).

4. 'Government culture cash drops.' **The Toronto Star**, September 26, 1997, Section C13. Although government expenditure on culture has been dropping steadily from 1990-1991 to 1995-1996, there are a few encouraging signs on the horizon. The federal government announced in 1997 that it would restore the $ 25 million taken from the budget of the Canada Council for the Arts.

5. Statistics Canada. **Focus on Culture: Quarterly Bulletin from the Culture Statistics Program.** Vol. 7. No. 3. Cat. # 87-004. Autumn 1995. Statistics Canada. Ottawa. 1995. p. 6.

6. Task Force on the Status of the Artist. **The Status of the Artist: Report of the Task Force.** Government of Canada. Ottawa. 1986.

7. **Ibid.** pp. 11-12 and 25-33.

8. The House of Commons of Canada. **Bill C-32: An Act to Amend the Copyright Act.** House of Commons. Ottawa. 1996.

9. 'Canada Book Day celebrates our literary best.' **The Toronto Star.** April 22, 1997. A 1.

10. 'Perfect time to figure out Canadian culture.' **The Toronto Star.** April 26, 1997. K 1 and K12. It should be emphasized that the statistics used in this article are national statistics. A different situation exists in Quebec due to a variety of linguistic, cultural and other factors.

11. See Department of Communications. **op. cit.** and Paul Audley. **op. cit.** for detailed statistics on foreign cultural programming and ownership of Canada's cultural industries.

12. Paul Audley. **op. cit.** pp. 11-65.

13. See for example: David Bell. **The Roots of Disunity: A Study of Canadian Political Culture.** Revised Edition. Oxford University Press. Toronto. 1992; Neil Bissoondath, **Selling Illusions: The Cult of Multiculturalism in Canada.** Penguin Books. Toronto. 1994; Richard Collins. **Culture, Communication and National Identity: The Case of Canadian Television.** University of Toronto Press. Toronto. 1990; Ramsay Cook. **Canada, Québec and the Uses of Nationalism.** 2nd. Edition, McClelland and Stewart. Toronto. 1995; Richard Gwyn. **Nationalism without Walls: The Unbearable Lightness of Being Canadian.**

McClelland and Stewart. New updated edition. Toronto. 1996; Carl James. **Seeing Ourselves: Exploring Race, Ethnicity and Culture**. Thompson Educational Publishing, Inc. Toronto. 1995; Kenneth McRoberts (ed.). **Beyond Quebec: Taking Stock of Canada.** McGill-Queen's University Press. Montreal and Toronto. 1995. David Taras, Beverly Rasporich and Eli Mandel. (eds.) **A Passion for Identity: Introduction to Canadian Studies.** Nelson Canada. Scarborough. 1993; Reginald Bibby. **The Bibby Report: Social Trends Canadian Style**. Stoddart. Toronto. 1995.

14. See for example: Task Force on Professional Training for the Cultural Sector in Canada. **Art is Never a Given.** Ministry of Supply and Services Canada. Ottawa. 1991. pp. 111-112. Also see Research and Evaluation Section. The Canada Council. **Artstats: Selected Statistics on the Arts and Culture in Canada.** 1st. edition. The Canada Council. Ottawa. 1993. (See Section One on : Estimated Size of the Cultural Sector).

15. William Littler. 'Budapest to Get a Taste of Canadian Culture.' **The Toronto Star.** February 1991. p. B5.

16. D. Paul Schafer. **The Character of Canadian Culture.** op. cit. pp. 4-50.

17. UNESCO. **A Practical Guide to the World Decade for Cultural Development 1988-1997.** UNESCO. Paris. 1987. p. 16 (insert mine).

18. Department of Communications. **op. cit.** p. 7. This understanding of Canadian culture owes much to the definition of culture endorsed by the members states of UNESCO at Mexico City in 1982. The UNESCO definition, in turn, owes much to the anthropological definition formulated by Edward Burnett Tylor a century earlier. In his publication **The Origins of Culture** which appeared in 1871, Tylor defined culture as "that complex whole which includes knowledge, belief, art, morals, custom, and any other capabilities and habits acquired by man as a member of society." (Edward Burnett Tylor. **The Origins of Culture.** Harper and Row Publishers. New York. 1958. p. 1).

CHAPTER IV

1. Bernard Ostry. **op. cit.** p. 204.

2. D. Paul Schafer. **Canadian Culture: Key to Canada's Future Development.** op. cit. pp. 17-27.

3. This metaphor of "culture as a tree" is very appropriate to the Canadian situation in view of the symbolic significance of trees for Canada and Canadians. The metaphor was first encountered by the author in a letter received from Dr. Min Jiayin of the Institute of Philosophy, Chinese Academy of Social Sciences, Beijing, China. For a more detailed treatment and graphic depiction of the metaphor of culture as a tree, see the presentations by Kalpana Das, Robert Vachon and Edward Hall in "Guswenta or the Intercultural Imperative." **Interculture.** Volume XXVIII. No. 2. Spring 1995/Issue #127. Intercultural Institute of Montreal. Montreal. 1995. pp. 52-53 and 56-57 respectively.

4. Jerry Diakiw. "The School's Role in Revealing the Commonplaces of Our National Culture and Identity: A Multicultural Perspective" in Keith A. McLeod (editor). **Multicultural Education: The Challenges and the Future.** (Multicultural Education: The State of the Art National Study. Report # 4). Canadian Association of Second Language Teachers. Winnipeg. 1996. pp. 26-39.

5. The Citizens' Forum on Canada's Future. **Report to the People and Government of Canada.** Ministry of Supply and Services Canada. Ottawa. 1991. pp. 74-85 and 163-164.

6. Canada. Department of National Health and Welfare. **Report of the Advisory Commission on Indian and Inuit Health Consultation.** Government of Canada. Ottawa. 1980. (Bergeron Commission) and Canada. **Royal Commission on Aboriginal People.** Government of Canada. Ottawa 1993. (Dussault-Erasmus Commission).

7. Jerry Diakiw. **op. cit.** pp. 32-33.

8. Jerry Diakiw. **op cit.** p. 32.

9. Jerry Diakiw. **op cit.** p. 32.

10. Jerry Diakiw. **op. cit.** pp. 29-36.

11. H. A. Giroux. "Curriculum, multiculturalism and the politics of identity." **National Association of Secondary Principals Bulletin.** 76 (548) 1992. p.7. Also see H. A. Giroux. "Living dangerously: Identity, politics and the new cultural racism." in L. Grossberg (ed.). **Between Borders.** Vintage Books. New York. 1993.

12. Seymour Martin Lipset. **op. cit.** p. 180.

13. Jerry Diakiw. **op. cit.** pp. 29-36

14. Citizens' Forum on Canada's Future. **op. cit.** pp. 34-50.

15. See for example: Canadian Tourism Commission. **Rediscover Canada: Year-Round Vacation Guide**. Canadian Tourism Commission. Ottawa. 1997; and Canadian Tourism Commission. **Canadian Heritage Discoveries.** Canadian Tourism Commission. Ottawa. 1997.

16. D. Paul Schafer. **Canadian Culture: Key to Canada's Future Development**. op. cit. pp. 29-53.

17. Joyce Zemans. "The Essential Role of National Cultural Institutions" in Kenneth McRoberts (ed.). **op. cit**. pp. 138-162.

18. **New Conversations: Exploring how culture sells the image of Canada abroad.** Report of a Conference on New Conversations convened in Halifax from June 9-11. 1995. p. 13.

19. 'Big Mountain' - Canada's Mark Rowswell, virtually unknown at home, is a star to millions of Chinese TV viewers.' **The Toronto Star.** People Section. Sunday. May 4. 1997. Section E. p. 1.

20. John Ralston Saul. **Culture and Foreign Policy. Canada's Foreign Policy: Principles and Priorities for the Future: The Position Papers.** Special Joint Committee of the Senate and of the House of Commons Reviewing Canadian Foreign Policy. Ottawa. November. 1994. p. 85.

21. For a fuller treatment of this subject, see D. Paul Schafer. **Canada's International Cultural Relations: Key to Canada's Role in the World.** World Culture Project. Markham. 1997.

22. The authority was Danny Newman of the Chicago Lyric Opera. While his theories and techniques were controversial at the time, in retrospect there can be no doubt that they contributed a great deal to the development of audiences and stabilization of the finances of many performing arts organizations in Canada. The costs of making Danny Newman available to arts organizations throughout the country were borne largely by the Canada Council.

23. See for example: Special Joint Committee of the Senate and of the House of Commons Reviewing Canadian Foreign Policy. **Report of the Special Joint Committee of the Senate and of the House of Commons Reviewing Canadian Foreign Policy.** Department of Foreign Affairs. Ottawa. 1994; and Government of Canada. **Canada in the World: Government Statement.** Canada Communication Group - Publishing, Public Works and Government Services Canada. Ottawa. 1995. A case is made in these documents for treating cultural relations as the "third pillar" in Canadian foreign policy alongside economic and political relations.

24. See D. Paul Schafer. "Cultures and economies: Irresistible forces encounter immovable objects." **Futures: The Journal of Forecasting, Planning and Policy.** Volume 26. Number 8. October. 1994. pp. 830-845 for a discussion of this.

25. D. Paul Schafer. "The Cultural Interpretation of History: Beacon of the Future" in Robin Blaser and Robert Dunham (ed.). **Art and Reality: A Casebook of Concern**. Talonbooks. Vancouver. 1986. pp. 167-186.

26. Karl J. Weintraub. **Visions of Culture: Voltaire, Guizot, Burckhardt, Lamprecht, Huizinga and Ortega y Gasset.** University of Chicago Press. Chicago. 1966. p. 219.

27. Much of the initiative for this will have to come from federal, provincial and municipal cultural departments, universities and community colleges with courses and programmes in cultural studies or cultural policy and administration, and organizations like the Canada Council for the Arts, Statistics Canada, the Canadian Conference of the Arts, the Association of Universities and Colleges of Canada, the Association of Canadian Community Colleges, the Canadian Bureau for International Education, the Centre for Cultural Management at the University of Waterloo, and others. The country needs effective models, tools, information and statistics to plan and develop Canadian culture in the future.

28. Robert Courchêne. "Teaching Canadian Culture: Teacher Preparation. " **TESL Canada Journal**. Vol. 13. No. 2. Spring 1996. pp 1-16. Also see Robert Courchêne. "What is Canadian Culture?" **The Converging of Two Visions: Proceedings of a Conference held at Glendon College, York University. May. 1995.** Canadian Scholars' Press Inc. Toronto. 1996. pp. 53-60.

29. Northrop Frye. **op. cit.** Also see James Polk (ed.). **Divisions on a Ground: Essays on Canadian Culture.** Anansi. Toronto. 1982.

30. Augustin Girard. **Cultural Development: Experience and Policies**. UNESCO. Paris. 1972. p. 137.

DESCRIPTION OF THE WORLD CULTURE PROJECT

The World Culture Project is a long-term research undertaking designed to promote the fact that culture has a crucial role to play in global development and world affairs. It is being undertaken to commemorate the World Decade for Cultural Development (1988-1997). For purposes of the Project, culture is defined in the holistic sense as worldview and values in general and a dynamic and organic whole in particular.

The Project has been subdivided into an International Component and a Canadian Component. The International Component is designed to develop the holistic concept of culture in broad, general terms, as well as to apply it to a series of complex and persistent global problems. The Canadian Component is designed to develop the holistic concept of culture in specific, practical terms, as well as to apply it to a similar set of Canadian problems. As a case study, the Canadian Component offers an unique opportunity to examine the theoretical and practical implications of the holistic concept of culture for a country which may be called upon to play a seminal role in the world of the future.

Consistent with the division of the Project into two basic components, a series of monographs is being developed for the International Component and the Canadian Component. A great deal of background research is undertaken in conjunction with each monograph and reactions are sought from advisory council members and authorities in the field. The topics of the monographs are:

INTERNATIONAL COMPONENT

The Character of Culture

The Politics of Culture

The Cultural Personality

The Community Culturescape

The Challenge of Cultural Development

Cultural Sovereignty and Change

International Cultural Relations

Cultural Education

Cultural History

Cultural Visions of the Future

CANADIAN COMPONENT

The Character of Canadian Culture

The Politics of Canadian Culture

The Canadian Personality

The Canadian Community Culturescape

The Challenge of Canadian Cultural Development

Canadian Cultural Sovereignty and Change

Canada's International Cultural Relations

Canadian Cultural Education

Canadian Cultural History

Visions of Canada's Cultural Future

For more information on the World Culture Project, please contact:

D. Paul Schafer
Director, World Culture Project
19 Sir Gawaine Place
Markham, Ontario
Canada, L3P 3A1
(905) 471-1342

ADVISORS TO THE CANADIAN COMPONENT
OF THE PROJECT

Greg Baeker	Toronto
André Fortier	Hull
Joy MacFadyen	Toronto
John Meisel	Kingston
Mavor Moore	Victoria
Walter Pitman	Toronto
Tom Symons	Peterborough
George Tillman	Ottawa
Steven Thorne	Kelowna
Paul Weinzweig	Victoria
Jiri Zuzanek	Waterloo